ADVERTISING CUTLERY

Richard D. White

Heating
HERCULES
Roofing
Home that you
our customers

NELSON BURBRINK
catcher ST. LOUIS CARDINALS
BOSTON
SOX

Advertising Cutlery

Richard D. White

Schiffer Publishing Ltd
4880 Lower Valley Road, Atglen, PA 19310 USA

Library of Congress Catalog Card Number: 98-88108

Book design by Blair Loughrey
Type set in Americana/Goudy Olst

ISBN: 0-7643-0738-x
Printed in China
1 2 3 4

This book is not sponsored, endorsed or otherwise affiliated with any of the manufacturers or other companies whose products are featured in this book. This book is derived from the author's independent research.

Published by Schiffer Publishing Ltd.
4880 Lower Valley Road
Atglen, PA 19310
Phone: (610) 593-1777; Fax: (610) 593-2002
E-mail: Schifferbk@aol.com
Please visit our web site catalog at **www.Schifferbooks.com**
or write for a free catalog .
This book may be purchased from the publisher.
Please include $3.95 for shipping.

In Europe, Schiffer books are distributed by
Bushwood Books
6 Marksbury Rd.
Kew Gardens
Surrey TW9 4JF England
Phone: 44 (0)181 392-8585; Fax: 44 (0)181 392-9876
E-mail: Bushwd@aol.com

Please try your bookstore first.

We are interested in hearing from authors
with book ideas on related subjects.

CONTENTS

ACKNOWLEDGEMENTS

People have always told me that I should be thinking about what I want to do after my eventual retirement. With this thought in mind, I decided that one of my "retirement" goals was to write a book about knives. I have managed to meet my goal prior to ending my career as a teacher, due largely to the encouragement of Mr. Peter Schiffer, of Schiffer Publishing, who read my original manuscript notes, evaluated my first photos, and called me on the phone, saying, "Richard, I like your idea...let's do it." Thanks also to Molly Higgins, my editor, for guiding me through this project and serving as my advocate during the publishing process.

This book would remain a dream, however, without the help of numerous enthusiastic knife collectors who gladly lent me advertising knives from their personal collections so that I could photograph them for inclusion into this book. The names of those supportive friends are: Nels Anderson, George Beckman, Lee Beene, Joe Bravo, Fred Clark, Charles Cole, Gene Corbin, Robert Dearing, Tom Gilroy, Corinne Grim, Mike Haggard, Robert Hansen, Marc and Pam Hill, Tom Hobson, Gordon and Roma Jack, Larry Jones, Warren Kothenbeutel, Dean Millar, Dave Miller, Byron Roderick, Randy Sipkema, Ron Smallwood, and Mark Zalesky. These individuals loaned me their personal knives to photograph, and also shared their personal knowledge, books, and other printed material dealing with advertising knives. With their collective enthusiasm, this book grew from an original estimate of 250 knife photographs to over 400. Several of these collectors met me at the flea market almost weekly, handing me recently purchased knives which they felt needed to be included in the book. Others carefully searched out advertising cutlery examples from their knife rolls and brought them to me during monthly knife club meetings, or sent packages of knives to me in the mail. Thanks to all of you.

A very special thanks to Barry Carithers, fellow educator, cutlery collector, writer, and confidant. Not only did Barry loan me numerous knives for inclusion into this book, but he has also been my "sounding board" throughout this project, bouncing ideas with me regarding various chapters, titles, and article ideas. On several occasions, Barry kindly became a knife transporter, from one of his collecting colleagues to me. After all of the knives were arranged into chapters and captions were written, Barry spent an afternoon evaluating knife prices, looking for inconsistencies, and checking cutlery production dates.

Finally, to Linda, my wife of over 20 years, a loving thanks for putting up with knives, camera gear, and manuscripts, spread out in small piles on the dining room table. As an English teacher, Linda looked over my shoulder; she volunteered to read my captions, check for word usage, sentence structure, and all the other things English teachers do so well. In addition, she assisted me in evaluating the composition of cutlery layouts, and helped lay out the various photographs into chapters. During those times when serious writing and research were underway, Linda kept the children occupied and out of Dad's hair. For my two children, Ashley and Shelby—thanks for helping arrange knives and photographs, and supporting Dad. This book is for both of you and your mother.

INTRODUCTION

Unlike other advertisement forms, the formal collecting of advertising cutlery is relatively new. This is the first publication devoted to providing detailed information about the various examples of cutlery produced as advertising "giveaways." As you browse through the various chapters, over 100 years of advertising history will unfold before your eyes.

Since thousands of companies used knives as the method of advertising various products, there has been no attempt to photograph even a significant portion of all advertising knives known to be in existence. In fact, each state in the Union could probably provide enough examples of advertising cutlery to fill its own good-sized publication.

Instead, the goal of this book is to provide photographic examples of well-known products, particularly interesting cutlery styles and shapes, and to explore the cutlery companies who produced these knives. This book takes not only a contemporary look at such advertisements, but a historical look as well.

Many of the products advertised on these cutlery examples will be household names; others will advertise rather obscure products or services. For many of these companies, advertising cutlery was only one of numerous products which were distributed to customers—both as a way of keeping the product name "on the tip of the tongue" and as a thank-you for being a loyal customer.

The goal of this book is not merely to provide a "photographic foray" into the colorful world of advertising cutlery, but also to educate the viewer to specific cutlery nomenclature and company histories. The captions beneath the photographs are, in most cases, rather extensive. They explain the various factors which have an effect on the overall value of each piece, including the condition of the knife, age, uniqueness, and cutlery design.

Hopefully, readers will sense the excitement of those who have donated knives to be photographed for this book. One of the intended benefits of this book will be the surfacing of many other examples of advertising cutlery stored for years in drawers and boxes and now made available for others to view and appreciate.

WHY PUBLISH A BOOK ON ADVERTISING CUTLERY?

Available Sources

For anyone with even a fleeting interest in collectible cutlery, there are fortunately several outstanding cutlery publications available on the market. All of these major publications are regularly updated, provide specific pricing information, and are extremely well-illustrated with numerous photographs and line drawings of all types of cutlery styles. In addition, these publications document the specific histories of most of the major cutlery companies which produced the vast majority of knives over the last 100 plus years. Furthermore, these publications give the reader the necessary knowledge to decipher the very informative "tang" portion of the knife's master blade—the small, unsharpened area near the base of the blade near the handle. Cutlery companies almost universally stamped the tang with the company name, often including codes to designate a particular knife's style, number of blades, handle material and production date(s). The cutlery books listed in the bibliography at the end of this book can be very helpful in the interpretation of these codes and stampings.

Although these publications, taken as a group or individually, reveal the knowledge gleaned from many years spent writing, researching, and collecting various forms of cutlery, they have generally overlooked *the use of cutlery as a viable mechanism for promoting various products through advertising.*

If you carefully examine the photographs illustrated in these various publications, you will find rare instances of advertising knives shown as a part of a particular knife brand. For example, in those publications which showcase the Remington Cutlery Company, you will see individual photographs of advertising pocketknives produced by Remington for such companies as Purina, Nehi, Franklin Fire Insurance, and Kelly Tires. Bernard Levine, in his *Guide to Knives and Their Values*, devotes a full page to Coca-Cola advertising knives and bartender and champagne style knives advertising various liquors, beers, and alcoholic products. Although these are significant starting points, the general subject of advertising cutlery has not been explored in detail.

Recent Trends

The recent proliferation of outstanding publications dealing with the subject of cutlery compares to a similar trend of books on specific advertising collectibles. The ever-increasing number of dealers at major antique shows who specialize in advertising collectibles and memorabilia is a distinct measure of the sudden rise in collectible advertising's popularity. Each of these factors have been attributed in part to the significant population of "baby boomers" who suddenly find themselves searching for remembrances of their youth. Taken together, these observations point to the need for a book which explores, in a comprehensive way, the use of cutlery as an advertising media.

Not only are advertising cutlery examples generally missing from cutlery books and publications, they are also missing from publications which deal with advertising collectibles. A thorough examination of most of the major publications which dealing with collectible advertising serves only to reinforce the general lack of information about the literally thousands of advertising knives produced during this last 100 years, their values, and place in the scheme of advertising giveaways.

For the person fortunate enough to stumble upon one of these advertising treasures, the unanswered questions are numerous. Generally, how much is the knife worth, and is it worth purchasing? Which bears greater weight in regard to value and collectibility, the condition of the knife or the advertising imprinted on it? Are advertising knives worth more or less than similar knives without advertising? Are advertising knives presently undervalued with the potential of significant appreciation in the future? What is the relationship between the knife maker or cutlery company and specific advertising? Finally, how does cutlery fit into the general scheme of advertising in the United States?

As I attend antique shows which specialize in advertising collectibles and antiques, I spend a great deal of time searching out examples of advertising cutlery. Much to my dismay, I have found that most dealers simply stay away from purchasing advertising cutlery, or if they find an advertising knife in a box as a part of an estate, they do not put it out for possible sale. The reason, I am told, is that there is no publication which is devoted to advertising cutlery which helps the dealer and collector answer these important questions dealing with value, brand name, condition, and price in a formal way.

Through literally hundreds of examples that have been carefully researched, arranged, priced, and photographed in color, this publication is designed not only to be visually striking, but to serve as a standard in the area of advertising cutlery.

ESTABLISHING THE VALUE OF ADVERTISING CUTLERY

In addition to displaying various advertising cutlery examples and providing a historical perspective of cutlery's place in the advertising arena, this book will provide a framework for evaluating the monetary value of similar forms of advertising pocketknives.

Naturally, at least some readers will have little or no background in examining and evaluating cutlery for purposes of setting potential value. It would be useful to review the accepted methods and factors normally used to evaluate regular pocketknives before proceeding to a system which can be used to evaluate knives bearing specific types of advertising.

The system for evaluating pocketknives in general is well-established and expanded upon in a number of publications already in print. Although they are similar, each publication varies slightly given each of the five major factors presented below. For example, some authors may give slightly more weight to the importance of a particular brand name over others, giving a company "4 stars" instead of "5 stars." Other points of minor disagreement center around what "defects" should be included or excluded when talking about the condition of the knife, or whether a "whittler" style is more desirable than a "muskrat" or "trapper" style of knife.

Regardless of these minor differences in descriptions and interpretations, I believe that all authors would agree that the five most important factors taken into account when examining a knife would include those listed below, although each author might rank these factors in a slightly different order of importance. These biases might be explained by personal preferences, experiences, and even geographical location of the authors.

The five factors which affect the overall value of any collectible cutlery are: CONDITION, BRAND NAME, STYLE, HANDLE MATERIAL, AGE.

Condition

Of these five factors used in determining overall value, condition is perhaps the most important consideration. Pocketknives, like most other items we now classify as "antiques" or "collectibles," were produced by a company and purchased by a consumer for a specific utilitarian purpose. Whether the products were crocks, tools, furniture, containers, toys, fishing lures, pens, or jewelry, most—if not all—items we now consider collectible were used on a daily basis, without regard for potential value to future generations.

Unfortunately, for today's collector, many of these items were "used up" through daily use. If not used up, they were cracked or broken in use, moving, or storage. The pocketknife is an obvious example. With the cutting of twine, sharpening of sticks, opening of boxes, prying, cleaning, punching, snipping, and most of all sharpening, the blades of knives were ground away, broken off, or sharpened into needlelike dagger points. In fact, most knife owners took great pride in sharpening their knives so that they would slice a tomato without denting the surface of the fruit. For many of these proud knife owners, sharpening a knife on a whetstone and "whittlin'" was part of the daily ritual which took place on a bench in the town square, talking to other country gentlemen.

In addition to the blades themselves being sharpened away, the working part of the pocketknife was often worn out through lack of maintenance. Pocketknife blades are designed and built at the factory to snap open and closed, and to stay firmly in the open position while in use. They achieve this snap (called the "walk and talk" in the knife business) by forcing the metal backspring to bend when the blade is open. After bending, the spring snaps back to place as the rounded end of the blade reaches the end of the rounded pivot.

To maintain this "blade action," and prevent unnecessary wear, the pocketknife owner must apply a drop of oil between the rounded blade end and the backspring so that the two pieces of metal do not grind against each other. Without this oil, the two metal pieces, held in tension against each other, wear down quite quickly, causing the blade to loose its snap. Interestingly, although knife carriers spent a significant amount of time making sure that their blades were razor sharp, (probably using a bit of oil on the stone as a sharpening aide), they frequently failed to put just a drop of oil on the ends of the knife to avoid the inevitable wearing of the rounded blade pivot.

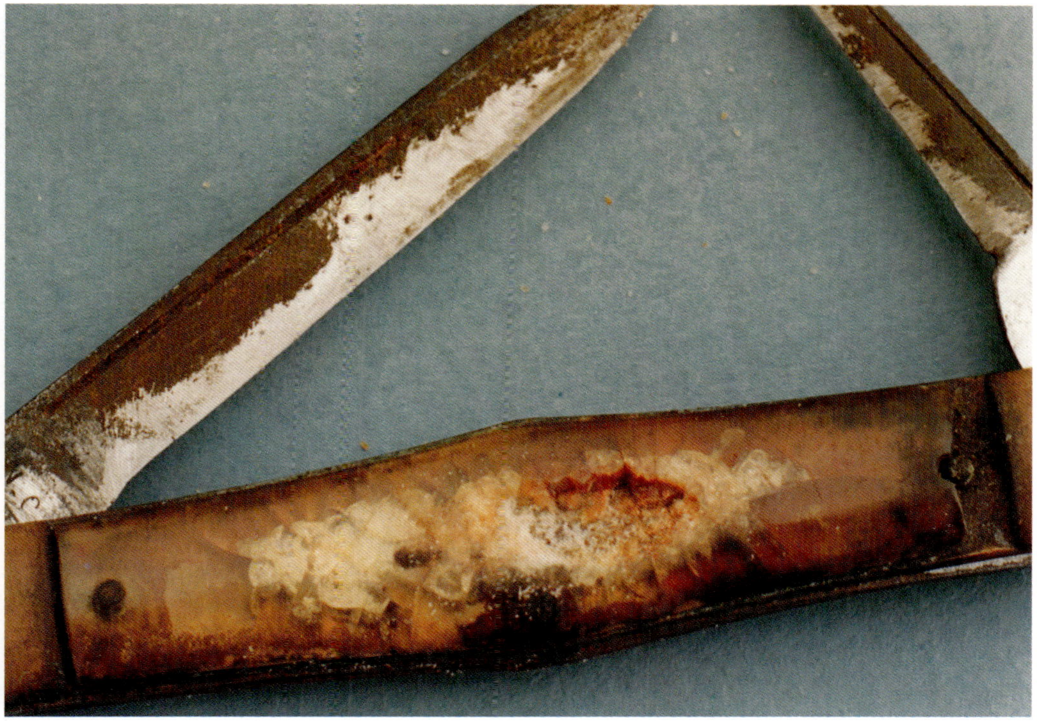

Although celluloid proved to be the perfect background material for the placement of various advertisements on cutlery pieces, celluloid had at least one disadvantage. This closeup photograph shows the extremely destructive nature of disintegrating celluloid and its effects on steel blades. Once this process has started, it is impossible to reverse. Owners of celluloid advertising knives should be aware of the potential breakdown of this material.

In addition, knife handles (called "scales") are frequently broken through abuse, dropping, or through the breakdown of the handles themselves. Although infrequently used in advertising cutlery, pearl and bone handles are frequently found broken on pocketknives.

Of greater concern to advertising pocketknife fanciers is the breakdown of the celluloid sides of advertising pieces. Celluloid, the first synthetic plastic made from cellulose nitrate, camphor, and alcohol, was invented in the early 1870s. As a handle material for advertising cutlery, it was almost perfect. It could be formed and shaped, made in a variety of colors, or made perfectly transparent so that an advertisement could be placed beneath it on the handle of a pocket or sheath knife.

Celluloid's downfall was its tendency to break down over the years, and become fragile and unstable if stored improperly. In fact, celluloid actually gives off a "gas" when it starts to disintegrate—turning all of the surrounding metal parts into a rusty mess. One celluloid knife which has started to break down can cause all of the other knives in the same knife roll to rust beyond repair, destroying the value of all. In spite of these conditions, however, celluloid-handled knives with both colorful handles and clear advertisements are highly in demand. Strong advertisements and pictures on these knives are most eagerly sought-after.

For the collector of celluloid-handled knives, the best precaution for successful storage of celluloid knives is to avoid storing them in airtight bags as this hastens the breakdown process. Another precaution is to avoid getting oil on the handles themselves, and to properly store the knives with a desiccant package for soaking up humidity.

The best general advice for knife owners is to examine these knives fairly regularly and remove all signs of rust. Separate all celluloid-handled knives showing the first signs of disintegrating from the rest of the collection. Additionally, most collectors wipe down the blade of knives with a soft cloth to deter rust from forming, or apply an extremely thin coat of oil on the blades in the hope that this film will prevent rust particles from adhering to the metal. Most importantly, remove all fingerprints from knife blades after handling, as fingerprints themselves contain a mild acid which actually etches the surface of metal.

For the collector, knives (including advertising knives) with the potential to increase in value are those that have *full blades which snap open and closed, handles in good condition (no cracks in the bone or breakdown of the celluloid), and which contain advertisements which are readable and in good condition* . Obviously, knives in mint condition are most desirable, and command the greatest prices.

Brand Name

Running a very close second to condition in terms of determining value is the brand name or "tang stamp." At the rear of the master blade, on the unsharpened flat part, almost all knife makers place their brand name or tang stamp. Because this area is protected from use and sharpening, even knives which are over one hundred years old and are totally worn out will still have very readable tang stamps. In addition to the specific name of the knife producer, this "tang" or unsharpened area gives, in many cases, specific information about when the knife was produced. The W. R. Case Cutlery Company, for example, uses a very sophisticated system of "dots" and slight changes in the company insignias, which can be interpreted by consulting a chart of production dates of specific knife styles.

In addition to the company name stamped on the tang, many knife companies use a numbering system which describes a series of valuable pieces of information about the knife. Often, these numbers are stamped on the opposite side of the tang from the company name, or appear on blades other than the master blade. Case, Remington, Keen Kutter, Schrade, and a number of other important knife companies used a combination of letters and numbers to indicate such things as handle material, number of blades, knife style, and steel types. For example, the W. R. Case Cutlery Company in Bradford, Pennsylvania produced an unusual knife known as an "elephant's toenail": a large, heavy knife which looks like its name. The Case designation for this knife with bone handles is "6250." The "6" is Case's designation for bone handles, the "2" is Case's designation for two blades, and the "50" is Case's designation for a style known as an "elephant's toenail." If you tell a collector you have a "Case 6250," he knows just what brand, style, handle material, and number of blades the knife has.

Getting to know these numbers, or at least knowing that they exist and can be researched, will enlighten even the most novice of knife collectors. They will assist the collector in knowing the age of the knife, and whether the handle material and blade styles are the correct ones for the particular knife in question. In most cases, the purchaser of a particular antique is matching his knowledge against a "professional dealer" who makes a living researching the value of various antiques and pricing them to make a profit. The advantage for the purchaser or collector, however, is that with the wide spectrum of antiques on the market, the normal dealer cannot become an expert in every antique. That's where specialty collectors prevail. Remember, informed collectors make wise decisions.

Perhaps more than any other type of antique, the company name stamped into the blade tang determines the value of the knife to a large extent. For those interested in finding out about a particular knife company, most major cutlery publications list all of the known knife makers in the world, with emphasis on the United States, and show the years of production and location of the cutlery company. Research into the formation of the American cutlery industry is a fascinating study indeed, because of its relationship to the development of American industry in general, and its parallel to the migration of immigrants to the United States from Great Britain and other cutlery-producing countries.

In these various knife publications, the various knife manufacturers are ranked by their value. These values are determined by the following factors: the production dates of the cutlery company (age), actual years of knife production (rarity), overall quality of the products produced, and the popularity of the product with consumers (geographical preference).

Some of the more popular cutlery companies are recognizable to all those who are involved in antiques. Names like Remington, Winchester, Case, Keen Kutter, Shapleigh Hardware, and Schrade are certainly familiar brands. Other tang stampings, however, are not as well-known.

All other conditions being equal, a knife with a good "pedigree" will be priced significantly higher than a similar knife with a stamping which does not rate as high.

For example, Purina contracted with several cutlery companies to make the famous "checkerboard" advertising knife. Most were made by Kutmaster, a tang stamping of the Utica Cutlery Company after 1937. These three-bladed knives are valued in mint condition at about $40.00. The same knife made on contract by Remington Cutlery is worth approximately $250.00—approximately six times more. Why? Because Remington, as a cutlery company, has a much higher ranking, brand recognition, and value to collectors who eagerly seek Remington knives. This is

The term "tang stamp" is widely used among knife collectors and experts. The tang of a knife is the unsharpened end of the master blade, the spot where the company name is stamped. Since this area is unsharpened and unused, the name stamped into the blade is virtually indestructible, and gives valuable clues to the maker, age of the knife, and potential value. This tang stamp indicates that this knife was made by the Utica Cutlery Company, located in Utica, New York. Utica used this early curved stamping from as early as 1910 to about the 1940s, thus helping to date a particular advertisement found on the knife.

due in part to the limited number of years in which Remington produced knives. Although they produced as many as 10,000 knives per day during the early 1930s, they were in production for only about 20 years.

Style

In every systematic evaluation of pocketknife values, style plays an extremely important part. Most pocketknives were originally designed to be used for a specific purpose.

These specialized purposes necessitated special blade configurations and blade shapes. An obvious example is a knife style called the "muskrat." The muskrat style was developed for use by trappers who skinned muskrats and other small fur-bearing animals. This knife had very long and narrow blades opposite from each other.

This shape was developed so that trappers could properly separate the skin from the bodies of these animals after trapping. No other knife had a blade style and configuration just like the muskrat. In addition, some followers of knife trivia think the name "muskrat" was given to this knife because the long slender blades looked like muskrat tails. Because of its unique style and shape, the muskrat is very collectible and sought-after by avid knife collectors.

In addition to the muskrat, many other pocketknife styles were named after the purpose for which they were designed. These names have included the folding hunter, cattle pattern, stockman, whittler, melon tester, fish knife, pruner, cotton sampler, and sailor's rope knife. All of these knife styles give a hint as to their original designed purpose.

In cutlery collecting and pricing, some general rules seem to hold true. First, in most cases, the larger the knife, the more valuable it has become. Almost without exception, the larger knife styles like folding hunters, cokebottles, lockbacks, and premium stockmen are priced higher than smaller equal end pens and jack knives. With advertising knives, however, there is one example which tends to go against the "larger is better" rule. This exception is the "melon tester," or "sausage knife."

Melon testers are extremely long and thin, designed to cut deeply into hams and melons for product testing. In spite of their length of almost five inches, they are generally a less expensive knife than other smaller varieties. This is largely due to the inexpensive construction of melon testers rather than their significant length.

In most cases, however, those "special purpose" knives are generally ranked higher than ordinary models. A good example is once again the elephant's toenail, also called the "Old English rope knife" or "sunfish." This massive double-ended jack knife is large and flat with thick stubby blades and massively wide backspring. It was used by surveyors to split stakes or by sailors to cut large ropes on ships. In both cases, the knife was placed on the log or rope and struck by a wooden-headed mallet. This knife is, because of its shape and rarity, highly valued and prized by collectors.

In the case of advertising cutlery, style plays a smaller part than in other forms of cutlery collecting. Almost without exception, advertising pieces are found on smaller, equal end pen knives or similar pieces. Since these knives were designed to be given away by merchants, smaller knives would be less expensive to produce, and were more likely to end up in the pockets of customers who would use them on a day-to-day basis.

Handle Material

Although knives can be found with a variety of handle materials, some are certainly preferred by collectors of fine cutlery. The "ranking" of handle materials from most to least desirable is as follows: pearl, genuine stag, ivory (rare), jigged bone, genuine tortoise (rare), fancy celluloids, nickel silver, ebony, buffalo horn, micarta, and delrin (modern moldable plastic). This list is subject to the particular likes and dislikes of individual collectors, as many cutlery collectors specialize in only one type of handle material, or collect a particular cutlery brand name known to use predominately one type of material for their handles.

Almost all high-quality *advertising* knives were handled in one of three identifiable celluloids. These were known as "cracked-ice," "waterfall" and "french ivory." All of these celluloids are light in color, either white or light yellow, and made perfect backgrounds for the etching or imprinting of various forms of advertising. In addition, the celluloids themselves had special visual characteristics, which made them not only functional but additionally beautiful as a background for the advertisement. The first, cracked-ice, was made in pure white or a very light yellow. Because of the manufacturing process, this celluloid has various lines and refractory inclusions which look like the lines of crystallized water seen running beneath the ice in a frozen pond.

The second, waterfall celluloid, is a manufacturing mystery. Although its appearance is a pale yellow or "mocha" color, it has various swirls or lines built into the celluloid. When turning a piece of waterfall from side to side, these lines and swirls seem to move or change places in the celluloid, much like the movement of water in a pond or waterfall. Although some of these early celluloids have been recently produced, waterfall has yet to be duplicated with modern production methods. The last celluloid used is called french ivory. Made to look like elephant ivory, this celluloid has lines running through it like the grain on real elephant ivory. This celluloid became the favorite of the florist industry, who used this celluloid extensively on advertising knives.

In addition, clear celluloid was often used to cover a picture or advertisement and was used in great quantities by four major cutlery companies: Golden Rule Cutlery Company, Aerial Cutlery Company, Novelty Cutlery, and Canton Cutlery. Knives made by these companies are so marked on the tang, and are desirable in good condition. Often the specific advertisement and address was placed on one side, and a wildlife scene, locomotive, political symbol, or other lithograph was placed on the other side.

Because of the tendency of celluloid to disintegrate over time, and because of the fading and discoloration of the covered photo or lithograph under the celluloid, outstanding examples of these picture knives are now in demand. They were made from about 1900 to the early 1930s.

Many of the older original advertising knives can also be found with nickel silver sides (scales) which are perfect for engraving, etching, and enameling. These metal sides could be polished to a high gloss or left with various "brushlike" surfaces. The majority of advertising knives made in Sheffield, England used nickel silver as the handle material on advertising knives.

Advertising knives can be found on rare occasions with the advertisement etched in a genuine pearl handle. Perhaps the most famous of these knives is the Remington doctor's knife etched "Mentholateum"—apparently a giveaway to doctors by the maker of this famous medicated grease. In addition, at least one example of the Purina advertisement can be found on pearl-sided knives made by Remington. These are extremely rare and difficult to find. Pearl, as a handle material, is beautiful but quite fragile. Its use was generally limited to smaller pen knives.

Age

For the collector of advertising cutlery, the age of the knife is a most important consideration. One easy way to determine the age of a piece of cutlery is to examine the name stamped on the tang of the master blade, and then refer to the knife company directory found in several cutlery publications. These publications will give you the production years of a particular knife brand. With cutlery companies which have been in business for 50 to 100 years, like Colonial and Imperial, however, additional methods of tracking down the age of the knife must be used.

Perhaps a better way to determine the age of an advertising specimen is to examine the advertising itself. In many cases, the advertising tells you the age of the cutlery. Some obvious examples of these interpretative dates include the various World's Fair knives that specifically tell you the years for which the knife was produced.

Other examples force the collector to do some "detective" work. By examining the pictures included in the advertising, patent numbers, appearance of the automobiles, terms, slogans, addresses and telephone numbers, the patient collector can approximate the date of the knife.

A good example, located pictorially in this book, is the raised-design metal pen knife given out by the Metropolitan Life Insurance Company of New York City. The picture of the building is surrounded by the caption "Tallest Building in the World." When one thinks of the tallest building in the world, the World Trade Center, the Empire State Building, or the Chicago Sears Tower immediately come to mind. Further research on the history of skyscrapers, however, led me to a chart which showed the comparative heights of the various skyscrapers in New York City and the completion dates of each building. The Metropolitan Life Insurance Building was, in fact, the tallest building in the world for only four years, from 1909 to 1913, until the F. W. Woolworth Building surpassed it. Knowing this data, and by researching the information about the knife producer stamped into the knife tang, I knew that this knife was produced almost 100 years ago.

SPECIFIC EVALUATION & PRICING OF ADVERTISING KNIVES

Using the five factors discussed above, a collector or dealer can narrow down the value of the knife based upon research of the tang stamp, and evaluating the overall condition of the knife.

With a general framework for evaluating knives in place, it is necessary to develop a scheme for those knives which were used by companies to showcase specific products.

Specific advertising cutlery pieces should be individually evaluated while weighing several significant factors.

Artwork

The first factor is the artwork which decorates the knife itself. The use of color schemes, inlays, embossed or engraved letters or objects, and the use of actual photographs all add to the value of the advertising piece.

One of my favorite groups of advertising are the engraved metal knives with unique shapes found in the whiskey advertisers. They are often found with enameled inlays and decorative swirls—almost as if the form and shape of the knife have been integrated into the function. They have been a favorite of collectors for years; the prices advertised for these pieces reflect their popularity.

A personal favorite is the bright checkerboard pattern found on the sides of Purina giveaway knives. These knives were produced for Purina, and feature striking red and white checks which instantly identify the product, even without reading the word "Purina" imprinted within the checkerboard design.

Remember that advertising knives were generally given out to loyal customers in return for patronizing a particular company. Given this factor, advertising knives were usually mass-produced in order to keep the cost per knife low. It is, therefore, a fortunate accident when a collector finds an advertising knife with unique and beautiful artwork or design in addition to an interesting advertisement. Add to this a knife which is in outstanding condition, made by a well-known company, and the combination is truly outstanding.

Historical Significance

The second factor in evaluating advertising pieces is the historical significance of the advertisement itself. Advertising knives which proclaim the attributes of Nehi Soda, Brown Shoes, or DeSoto Automobiles are historically important as they speak of products which are presently not on the marketplace.

Those advertising pocketknives which will command the highest prices are those which were produced during the heyday of advertising in the United States, from the turn of the century until the early 1950s. During this time, knives were only one of thousands of advertising objects which were given away to loyal customers.

World's Fair knives are of special historical significance, and specially produced knives were only one of many special souvenir items produced for these events. In some instances, several different cutlery companies produced knives for a particular World's Fair. As a collectible, these knives, and anything else associated with these events, take on a particular significance, and are sure to increase in value.

Another important historical event are those advertising knives which are special commemoratives. In particular, those knives which celebrate the 100th year anniversary of the company are especially sought-after. Also important are those knives which commemorate a particularly important event with national or international significance.

The historical significance of those knives which were produced for various fraternal organizations is not to be overlooked. In some cases, these fraternal organizations represented a particular social phenomena or outlook. A good example is the original Ku Klux Klan knife produced by New York Knife Company in the 1920s.

Those knives produced in the 1960s to 1980s are generally not as valuable as earlier pieces, nor are those advertising knives which are reproductions of earlier examples (Coca-Cola, for example). These knives are often made overseas, with cheap labor and cheap materials. The purchaser must be aware of such reproductions, by closely examining the product, and familiarizing yourself with production dates and specific characteristics of the knife. Like other antiques, if it looks too good to be an original, then it probably isn't.

Featured Product

The third factor which determines the value of advertising cutlery is the featured product on the knife itself. For the advertising collector, this may be the most important factor. Some collectors collect all advertising in general, others collect different advertising companies printed on a common vehicle (like calendars, ashtrays, tins, etc.), while others seek out all examples of advertising which have a particular brand name.

The most popular consumer product of all time is undoubtedly Coca-Cola. The Coca-Cola Company has issued literally hundreds of various advertising products, including advertising knives which have been eagerly snatched up by loyal consumers. Large collecting clubs have been formed, and several outstanding guides have been published for this specific company. In addition to Coca-Cola, there are a number of other products which have significant consumer loyalty and whose advertising products command high prices. The list of these products includes: Anheuser-Busch, Cracker Jack, Planters, Mr. Peanut, Morton Salt, Sunshine Biscuits, De Laval Cream Separators, Wrigley, Quaker Oats, Campbell Soups, R. J. Reynolds, Buster Brown, Hires, and Pepsi-Cola, to name just a few of the most popular ones.

Knives with these most popular advertisements will appeal not only to the knife fancier, but also to the specific advertising collector. In terms of determining value, the advertising pieces which have been produced *during the period of greatest advertising activity* will command the top prices.

Unique Shapes

Knives which have unique shapes have been desirable commodities even from the beginnings of knife collecting. The most famous and popular shape has been the "shoe knife" or "leg knife," used by a number of companies almost since the inception of advertising cutlery. Perhaps the most prolific of the companies to use the leg knife in its advertising has been the Brown Shoe Company. Brown Shoe shoe knives are extremely rare, and popular with all collectors. Brown Shoe knives sometimes have a nickel silver shoe and a colored celluloid "leg" or sock portion, or were made with a single bright celluloid "sock" covering the entire knife. In rare cases, two contrasting celluloids were joined together to form the total shoe. The contrast between these two materials is striking and the use of this design is truly a cutlery innovation.

In addition to shoe knives, advertising cutlery pieces have been designed to look like baseball bats, vehicles, guns, planes, cucumbers, bottles, and many other product shapes. There are some collectors who specialize in these fancy figurals alone. Having an interesting advertisement engraved on the side only adds to the interest and value. Take your time examining these uniquely shaped knives. Although the unique shape prompts the potential purchaser to buy without looking closely, often, because of their delicate shape, these knives have suffered some damage around the pin areas which will decrease their overall value.

Hopefully, with these guidelines, some specific cutlery books, and the prices shown on the many examples included, this book will serve as a real resource for those interested in this fascinating area of historical advertising collecting.

THE KNIFE THAT STARTED IT ALL

Fittingly, my story begins in the South...in the heart of "knife country," where senior citizens still meet daily in the courthouse square to whittle, trade knives, and discuss the events of the nation.

Driving from Winston Salem, North Carolina to the mountainous regions near Boone, my wife and I found ourselves stopping at every flea market and sign that read "ANTIQUES." It was July, and the weather was typical for North Carolina: hot and extremely humid.

As I remember, we stopped frequently along the highway, sometimes backtracking, sometimes following signs that directed us down small side roads. The destination was frequently a large metal "quanset hut" type building which doubled as a local flea market and antique shop. Sometimes leaving the air-conditioned car made us wonder if the trip was really worth it, but the thought of finding an antique cutlery treasure provided enough of an incentive to lure us inside.

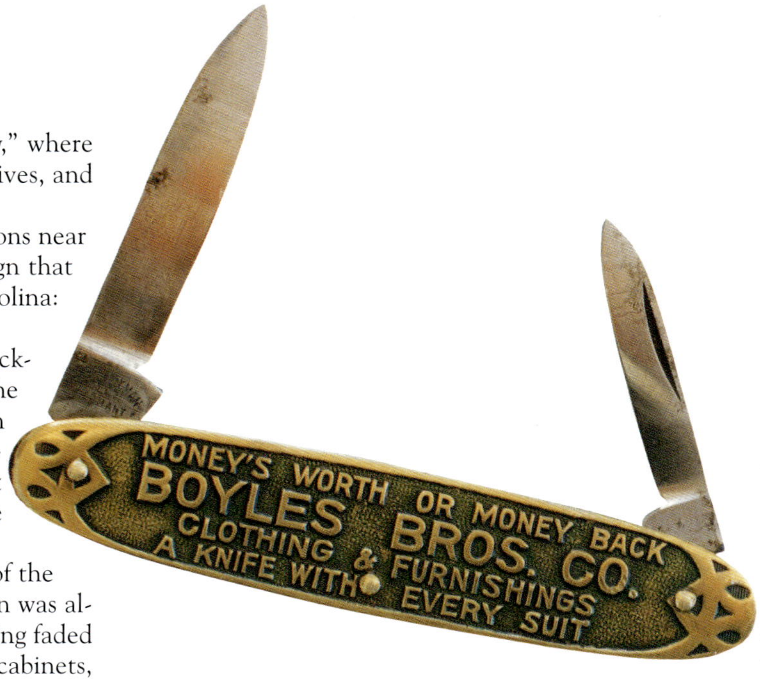

The engraved caption on this small, metal-sided pen knife was certainly intriguing. "A Knife With Every Suit," the caption proclaims. In addition, a second caption reads "Money's Worth or Money Back." With these two pronouncements, Boyle's Brothers Company sets the standard for customer satisfaction. This form of advertising, simple yet effective, sets the stage for a closer look at cutlery advertising.

One such visit found us in a large, hot, tin-roofed building, with most of the interior light coming from translucent skylights set in the roof. The question was always the same: "You folks have any old knives for sale?" A young man wearing faded blue jeans and a once-white t-shirt led me past rows of canning jars, metal cabinets, stacked tobacco baskets, and piles of old magazines to a locked showcase sitting high on an old wooden bookcase, the only possible source of old pocketknives in this particular building.

Opening the cabinet, the dealer invited me to rummage around in the assortment of old badges, bottle openers, toys, fountain pens, and such until I found a decent pocketknife. The knife was a "toothpick" style, with colored celluloid handles. The name stamped on the tang read "Imperial, Providence, R.I." After opening and closing the knife several times, inspecting the blade length, and checking for cracks in the celluloid, we quickly agreed on a price.

Knife in hand, I had just started to weave my way back towards the front of the building to pay for the purchase, when I heard the clerk say, rather matter-of-factly, "that's interesting, I thought you'd be more interested in this other knife." Having seen no other knife in the showcase, I turned to see what the clerk was holding in his hand. He held up what appeared to be a metal-sided pen knife with raised lettering on the sides.

Taking the knife from the clerk for closer evaluation, I read the advertising inscribed on both sides of the knife. "BOYLES BROS. CO. Clothing & Furnishings," the knife boldly proclaimed. What struck me, however, was not the name of the clothier, but the slogan which appeared below the company name. It read "A Knife With Every Suit." I realized why the clerk felt that this knife was significant to a knife collector. A Knife With Every Suit—what an interesting slogan. I assumed that Boyles Brothers would actually give each customer who purchased a suit a free knife. Apparently, this company felt that the promise of a free knife would entice the "man on the street" to buy a suit.

Further evaluation of the knife led me to the tang stamping which read "Antelope," another piece of information to fit into the puzzle. Intrigued by the story behind this particular metal-sided knife, I purchased the second knife as well.

Closer examination of this knife revealed that, in addition to the slogan "A Knife With Every Suit," this knife contained another piece of advertising. Above the company name, a second slogan was embossed: "Money's Worth or Money Back." This company was really trying to say something to the consumer. Taken together, the two slogans and the stamping on the blade would certainly be worth investigating.

If my memory served me correctly, the "Antelope" tang stamping was placed on knives during the 1920s to 1930s, during the Great Depression. During this time money was scarce, and the purchase of a new suit a memorable event—one in which other sacrifices had to be made. For most members of this thrifty generation, the possibility of receiving a useful knife might have been just the ticket to cement the decision.

Remember, for these citizens, a knife was not just a "giveaway" to be tossed into a drawer. Pocketknives could be found in almost everyone's pockets, ready to open a package, cut a piece of twine, sharpen a wooden pencil, clean dirty boots, or cut loose threads. A working man would rather leave his keys at home than leave the house without his pocketknife.

Knowing this, Boyles Brothers Suit Company made a wise decision to use pocketknives as advertising pieces, and to design a knife which was small enough to fit comfortably into a man's pocket without wearing a hole. Because of the small size, this knife could certainly be carried in a suit pants pocket, or claimed by a wife for use in a purse or sewing basket. Every time a man pulled the knife out of his pocket, the name Boyles Brothers would appear, and would be re-etched into his mind. Certainly, this company would be formost in the mind of a family the next time they contemplated the purchase of a suit. That's the power of advertising, and nobody did it better than Boyles Bros.

FUTURE TRENDS

The systematic exploration and evaluation of advertising cutlery is truly in its infancy. This publication is the first of its kind to explore this specialized form of advertising and develop a system of evaluating prices for different examples of advertising cutlery. As such, it is possible to "get in on the ground floor" in terms of searching out significant cutlery examples.

After talking to serious collectors in both the advertising and cutlery fields, some general suggestions and collecting trends have emerged. First, as in all fields of collecting, seek out those advertising cutlery examples which are in excellent or mint condition if possible. These pieces have the greatest chance of real appreciation.

Second, advertising imprinted on the sides of well-established cutlery names will appreciate at a faster rate than those from lesser known companies. Also, cutlery pieces which advertise nationally known products or famous products from yesteryear will remain in high demand.

Emerging as a possible item to look for are World's Fair knives, especially with the recent publication of an outstanding book on World's Fair items.

There has been in recent years a decline in farming acreage and a decrease in the number of individuals involved in farming, ranching and agriculture. Advertising knives which deal with agricultural seeds, cattle feeds, and farm equipment, especially knives that are well made, will continue to be in demand.

Brewery and tobacco advertising will become more valuable especially as tobacco legislation becomes more stringent. Interestingly, although hundreds of different products from neons to coasters advertise various beer and alcohol items in the last 50 years, very few used cutlery as a means of advertising. Special figurals, especially shoe and leg knives and baseball bats will continue to be popular, especially in good condition with celluloid intact. Also, champagne knives with corkscrews, metal sides and other specialty blades will become a more premium collectible.

Due to recent declining membership rosters, fraternal advertising knives will assume a more important role. Included are the International Order of Foresters, Shriners, Masons, and Odd Fellows, as well as Eagles, Moose, VFW, and others. Most of these knives are well-made by cutlery companies known for their quality products.

Metal-sided knives bearing advertising, generally overlooked for generations, are suddenly moving to the forefront. These well-made knives are engraved with a tremendous variety of advertisements, and because of the metal sides, have remained in good condition for years. Pick those in the best physical condition with full blades. Look for knives bearing advertising for products not available today like asbestos companies, fire insurance companies, and so on.

Sitting here reading my e-mail, it strikes me that, like the way we communicate with one another, the whole concept of consumer advertising has changed drastically in the last few years. As we approach the next century, multimedia blitzes will continue to become more dramatic and will dominate our visual and auditory senses.

For those who grew up in the 20th century, however, advertising items once given in appreciation of loyalty and recognition will be tangible reminders of products and services which operated with the customer in mind. These advertising items were, in real terms, the physical link between the merchant and the customer. As such, they will continue to be sought after as advertising moves to a more "impersonal" media approach.

1. AGRICULTURAL FEEDS, SEEDS & SERVICES

Above: These three-bladed small Purina stockman knives given away to customers who purchased Purina feed products are becoming truly a "blue ribbon" collectible. These are made by Kutmaster after 1937 to approximately 1960. There has been in the past several years a significant increase of interest in Purina knives. As an advertiser, they are perhaps the most recognizable advertising knife. Value in mint condition $40–50

Right: A closeup of three advertising knives made by Kutmaster. The top and bottom are for the famous Purina Company, with the slight differences in the color of the celluloid clearly shown. The middle knife, also very colorful, advertises "Supermoist," another cattle feed product. As a trio, these knives make outstanding additions to an advertising collection.

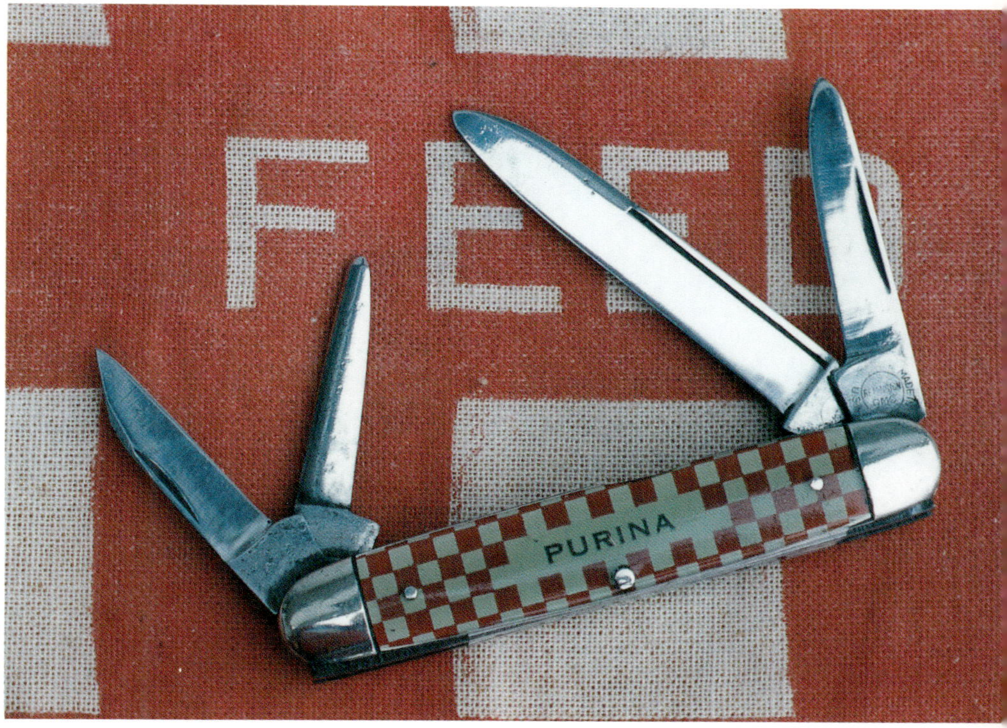

Top left: Close-up photographs of two Purina giveaways, produced by Kutmaster. Notice the two variations of colors on the checkerboard. One has white squares, the other almost a yellow color. Value $40–50 each in mint, unsharpened condition.

Left: Although the most frequently found Purina advertising knives found bear the Kutmaster tang stamping, this three-bladed cattle pattern bears the famous Remington Cutlery stamping on the master blade. Remington was purchased by Pal Cutlery in 1941, so this knife was probably made in the 1930s. This cattle pattern has, in addition to the master blade, a punch and a spey blade—all necessary blade styles for those involved in ranching and farming. Although the blades are full, the pitting and rust on the blades would lower the value of this knife to $125–150.

Top right: Perhaps the rarest of the Purina advertising knives is the Remington 4-bladed cattle pattern. Although worn from use, this knife still proudly bears the Purina advertising and familiar checkerboard design under its clear celluloid handles. Photographed on top of an original Purina cloth feed sack—itself a valuable antique—this knife would be worth $300 in excellent or near-mint condition. As is, the value is approximately half that, about $150.

Purina's Checkerboard Design Creates Well-Known Advertising Symbol

The company behind the famous checkerboard symbol, Purina Mills, recently celebrated its 100th year anniversary. Founded by William H. Danforth in 1894, the Purina Company (originally called the Robinson-Danforth Commission Company) was the result of a partnership which was formed to produce animal feed, and operate a retail feed store. Danforth's energy proved to be the key in pushing the young company forward into the next generation.

The use of the very famous checkerboard design is a story in itself. According to Purina history, the story dates back to the time when Danforth was a young boy growing up in Charleston, Missouri. As a helper in his father's general store, young Will watched various families come into town to purchase their weekly supplies. One large family stood apart from the rest. All of the members of this family wore clothing made of bright red and white checkerboard material. Supposedly, this brightly colored design would help the parents easily find their children as they played in the town square while their parents purchased supplies. Years later, Purina founder Danforth remembered this bright checkerboard pattern and chose it for his company's trademark.

The checkerboard trademark has been well-guarded for over 100 years. Although several other companies have tried over the years to use the checkerboard for their products, Purina has successfully blocked all attempts at having this famous symbol used by competitors.

The history of Purina includes several important milestones. First was the development of the word "Purina" in the early years. Literally, the word "purina" was an invented word, implying the pure state of the corn and oat mixture which went into the feeds. Second was the Purina display at the 1904 Louisiana Purchase Exposition World's Fair in St. Louis. At that fair, visitors were greeted by fifteen magnificent palaces which held treasures never seen by the public. Ralston-Purina's exhibit included the now-famous checkerboard in a building which housed examples of Ralston's cereal and feed products.

The third event was the use of the word "chow" in the Ralston feed line. "Chow" was the name given to food by soldiers in World War I. Even today, we speak of the "chow line" when we refer to soldiers waiting outside of the mess hall. Danforth felt that his cattle and cereal grains were not just food, but should instead be called "chow," as important a product as hot food to hungry soldiers. From that time on, the words Purina and Chow became constant companions.

In the thirties, during the Great Depression, Purina looked to other sources to try to solve sagging demand for its cereal products. They found their answer in a Hollywood hero—cowboy Tom Mix. Working with Purina, the western movie star helped to form the famous Tom Mix Ralston Straight Shooters Club. As a member of this special club, youngsters could send in box tops from Ralston Hot Cereal in exchange for Tom Mix's life story, cowboy bandana, and secret code ring. This advertising gimmick proved to be an overwhelming success with hundreds of thousands of kids sending in box tops. All of these advertising giveaways are collectible in their own right.

As a supporter of the United States' efforts in World War II, Purina challenged the farmers and ranchers of America to do their part in winning the war by producing food for the servicemen and women who were serving abroad As a part of this effort, salesmen visited farms to develop "action sheets" designed to assist the farmer produce better products with less spoilage and waste.

Purina has grown significantly in the past 103 years, now producing over 5 million tons of chow in 54 major plants all across this United States. In addition to cattle feed, Purina produces special feed products for hogs, calves, show steers, dairy cows, horses, birds, zoo animals, chicks and chickens, and other specialized animal needs. Purina supplied food for the sled dogs in the 1933 Robert Byrd expedition to Antarctica as well as being the primary food source for hundreds of champion race horses in Lexington, Kentucky. As the industry spread throughout the United States, Purina developed a comprehensive plan for training and educating the rural farmers and ranchers in the various methods of livestock feeding programs. Contests, conferences, visitation, publications, and rewards for achieving various goals were all a part of this public education program.

As a part of the massive advertising techniques designed to develop wholesale and retail accounts from feed stores, feed lots, farms and dairies Purina commissioned numerous products which were given to salesmen, customers, and owners of these feed companies, in return for new or enlarged accounts. Among the many products produced as incentives were brass scales for weighing milk, rings, clothespin bags, posters and signs, brass animals, fine art animal paintings, ties, and even real baby chickens. The company also gave away well-made pocketknives with the famous Purina name, the red and white checkerboard overlaid with clear celluloid on the sides of the handles. These checkerboard knives were originally made by at least two companies, Remington and Kutmaster. In later years, Utica and even Buck produced knives with the checkerboard pattern on the sides. The original Purina knives were made during the 1930s by Remington, and into the 1940s and 50s by Kutmaster.

As a collector item, the Remington Purina knives, produced in both a three- and four-bladed cattle pattern, have always retained their high value—in part due to the famous Remington stamping on the knife. These Remington Purina knives in both blade patterns can cost the potential collector over $200 for examples in mint condition. The Kutmaster knives, on the other hand, even though they have been made as far back as the early 1940s, have been overlooked for years, and are, in the opinion of some collectors, coming into their own as a cutlery collectible worth investing in. These Kutmaster Purina knives can still be found in mint condition, and are purchased reasonably in the $30 to $40 range. The Kutmaster Purina knives, made in a three-bladed small stockman pattern and a two-bladed pen knife, are a good quality knife with bright, clear advertising on both sides. They will, in my opinion, continue to increase in value in the coming years, as they are one of the only advertising knives to advertise a national company which has been in existence over 100 years.

Above: A comparison photo of three Purina advertising knives made by different companies. The upper left was made by Remington, the bottom left by Kutmaster, and the newest knife on the bottom right was made by the Utica Cutlery Company. The greenish cast of the Remington Purina's celluloid sides is noticeable alongside of the two other knives.

Above right: A recent entry into the Purina advertising cutlery is stamped on the tang "CCC, Canton, O." Upon first reading, this stamping would indicate a knife made by the Canton Cutlery Company. Canton Cutlery made "picture knives" with photos showing through clear celluloid. Canton was in business from 1879 to 1930. This knife, however, is recently, and inexpensively made. The center pin holding the knife together does not show, a characteristic of fine knives. The metal ends are held to the knife body by metal tabs crimped into the bolster. In addition, the "plastic" sides stick above the bolster ends. This is an interesting Purina advertising knife, and an excellent addition to such a collection. It has a value of $25–30.

Right: Purina contracts with various cutlery companies to produce a commemorative knife. In this case, Buck was the producer of this colorful lockback. Produced to be given out to special customers by feed and grain store owners, or by Purina salesmen to large corporate accounts, this knife is very rare. Like all Purina advertisers, it sports the famous checkerboard logo under clear plastic. Value is $35–40, because of its rarity, colorful advertising, mint condition, lockback, and famous Buck stamping.

Above left: When most people think of Purina, they think of cattle feed. Purina, however, made breakfast cereals as well. In order to promote these cereals, Purina sponsored Tom Mix, a famous Hollywood western star. Together, they founded the "Tom Mix Straight Shooters Club" during the 1930s. Children who joined this club received prizes for sending in cereal boxtops. This rare knife is one of those premiums. Stamped with both the Tom Mix brand in the Purina checkerboard, Tom Mix's name, and the Straight Shooters Club, this knife is a rare find. Made by the Quickpoint Cutlery Company, St. Louis, this knife features yellow cracked-ice celluloid handles and tip bolsters. Its value is $65–75, perhaps more because of the unique story which surrounds this knife.

Above right: Most of the common Purina knives are in the three-bladed small stockman pattern, made by Kutmaster. This two-bladed pen knife, also made by Kutmaster, is an exception. Still bearing the famous checkerboard symbol and bold Purina logo, this knife is in unsharpened mint condition. It is valued at $40–50.

Left: This blue plastic multiblade was given out by pet food distributors to customers who purchased Purina dog food. As seen on the master blade, this knife was made in China. Like others produced in the same country, it has no real cutlery value. Its value lies in its advertisement and possible utilitarian use. Value is $10–15.

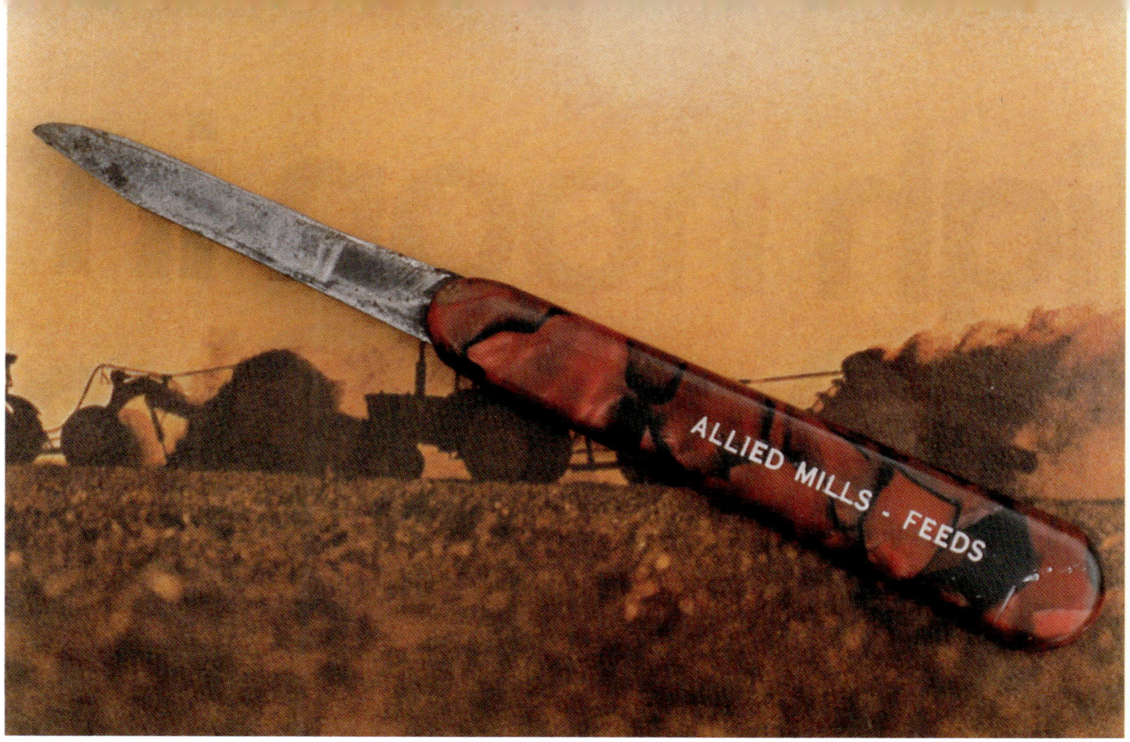

Right: This knife is called a "push blade," in which the blade slides into the knife handle. The blade is opened by pushing on a small tab which slides in a grove on the back side of the knife. "Allied Mills and Feeds" is the name imprinted on the celluloid handle. Although the knife is not in good shape, having been sharpened roughly, the name is well-imprinted, and contrasts sharply with the colorful handles. Value in this condition is $10.

Below left: "MoorMan's" is a company which produces cattle feeds. This three-bladed premium stockman is handled in "slick black" celluloid, rather rare for cutlery handles. The shield used to advertise the cattle feed product, again rare for advertising knives. Made by Camillus, in the 1960s, it is valued at $60–70 in its present mint condition.

Below right: This closeup of the MoorMan's advertising knife shows a closeup of the tang stamp on the master blade. This particular stamping with the word Camillus underlined was used after 1963; it would be called a "three line" stamping.

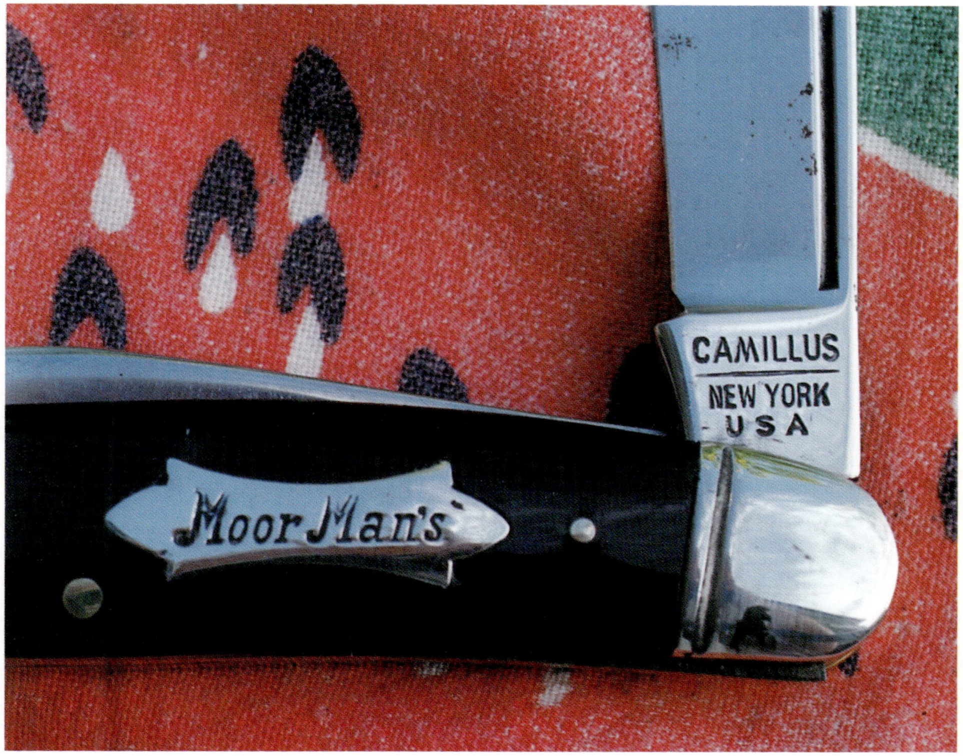

This rare agricultural advertising knife advertises "Supermoist Feeds," and was made by Kutmaster—probably in the 1940s or early 50s. The slanted stripes contrast with the "Supermoist" wording. Value $40–50 in mint condition.

This knife, advertising "Gooch's Best Feeds," was given away by feed and grain stores to customers who purchased cattle feeds. The Ambassador tang stamping indicates that the knife was made by the Colonial Cutlery Company, located in Providence, Rhode Island, probably in the 1960s. It is of low quality; the plastic advertisement is stuck onto the metal shell. The value is $10, perhaps up to $15 to agricultural advertising collectors.

Above left: This three-bladed premium stockman was made by Kutmaster. It advertises "Foxbilt Feeds," a company which produced cattle feeds. The company logo is clearly etched on the french ivory celluloid. Dating from the 1940s or early 1950s, this knife is a significant advertising collectible.

Above right: The rear panel of the Foxbilt Feeds stockman reveals the company slogan. Obviously, this knife was presented to owners of feed and seed stores in appreciation for purchase of large quantities of cattle feeds. Value is approximately $30–40 because of its slightly rough condition.

Left: This outstanding "Northrup Seeds" advertising cutlery piece, made by Kutmaster, is rare because it contains one blade more than the usual three blades normally found in the stockman knife pattern. Useful to farmers and ranchers, it contains a spey blade (for castrating), a sheepfoot blade, punch, and master blade. This knife is an illustration of a cutlery piece in pristine mint condition, and has a value of $55–65.

Above left: This "Northrup King Seeds" premium stockman is a smaller version of the four-bladed Northrup King Seeds advertising knife, but contains only three blades: a pen, spey, and master blade. Given to customers who purchased seeds, this premium stockman has a value of $40–45 because of its outstanding mint condition, age, and clear advertising.

Above right: A comparison of two sizes of Northrup King Seeds knives. Made by Kutmaster in the 1940s or early 1950s, the larger knife is almost 4″ in length, and the smaller 3 3/8″ in length.

Right: "Pioneer Seeds" is the advertisement on this 2-bladed jack made by Imperial Knife Company. Because it is known as a "shell handle" style, with a cheaper knife construction and a plastic sheet containing the advertisement wrapped around the thin metal handles, its mint condition increases the value of this knife to $20.

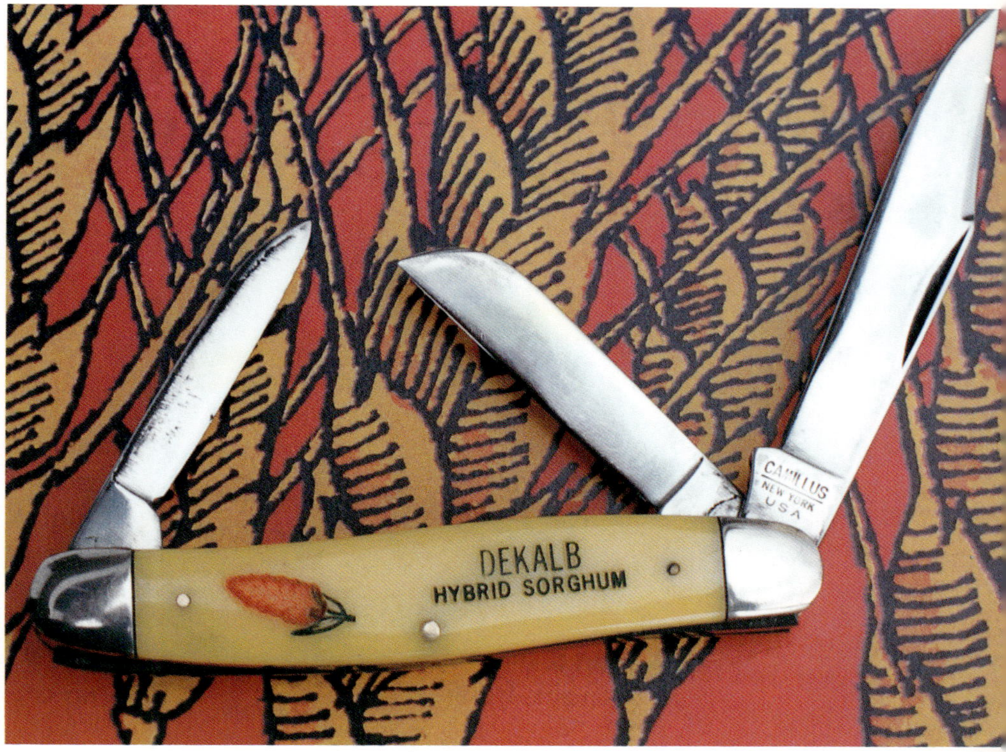

Above: "Trojan Seed Company" is the advertisement depicted on the sides of this shell-handled two-bladed jackknife. With bright red lettering and yellow corn background, this combination makes a striking advertiser. In spite of the fact that it is a cheaply made knife with the plastic celluloid stretched over a metal shell, it has a value of $10–15.

Above right: "Dekalb" is a familiar name to the rural community, most often seen as metal "winged corn" signs along country roads. Dekalb is one of the largest producers of agricultural seeds, primarily grown for animal feeds. This small three-bladed stockman is in near-mint condition, and was made by Camillus Cutlery sometime after 1963. Its bright yellow handles with etched and painted corn cob make this knife an excellent collectible. Probably given away by grain elevator operators, Dekalb salesmen, or owners of feed stores, it has a value of $40–50 in this condition.

Right: Strasburg, Colorado is a small farming community approximately thirty miles east of Denver on Interstate 70. This advertiser for "Kiowa Grain" is a shell-handled knife with the plastic advertising wrapped around the pre-formed metal sides. As such, its value is only as an advertiser. It was most certainly a giveaway to farmers and ranchers. Value is $10.

Left: This advertiser was produced around the turn of the century. Canton Cutlery started making picture knives in 1888 to around 1920. This advertiser encourages farmers to consign their grain to "E. E. Buxton of Memphis, Tennessee." The sheaves of wheat and good condition of the clear celluloid help this knife to have a value of $30. The poor condition of the blades lowers the overall price of the knife considerably, from a potential of $60 or higher. In addition to the Canton Cutlery Company, the other manufacturers of clear-handled picture knives were the Golden Rule Cutlery Company, the Novelty Cutlery, and the Aerial Cutlery Company.

Below left: This cattle feed advertiser is truly unique. Made by Kutmaster in the 1940s or early 1950s, its handle material is colorful on both sides. Interestingly, very few advertising knives were made using the "Barlow" pattern: this knife is an exception. The front of the knife shows a very patriotic red, white, and blue pattern with a white horse and rider silhouetted against the sunset.

Below: The rear panel of the Kutmaster Barlow shows the actual advertising. Set against striking red background are the words "Wayne Feeds" and "Wayne Animal Health Aids." The motto of these agricultural companies is also indicated: "Working Partners." Although the blades on this working man's knife are badly worn down through resharpening, this knife has a value of $30–40. It would certainly be a candidate for a blade restoration because of its unique and colorful two-sided advertising.

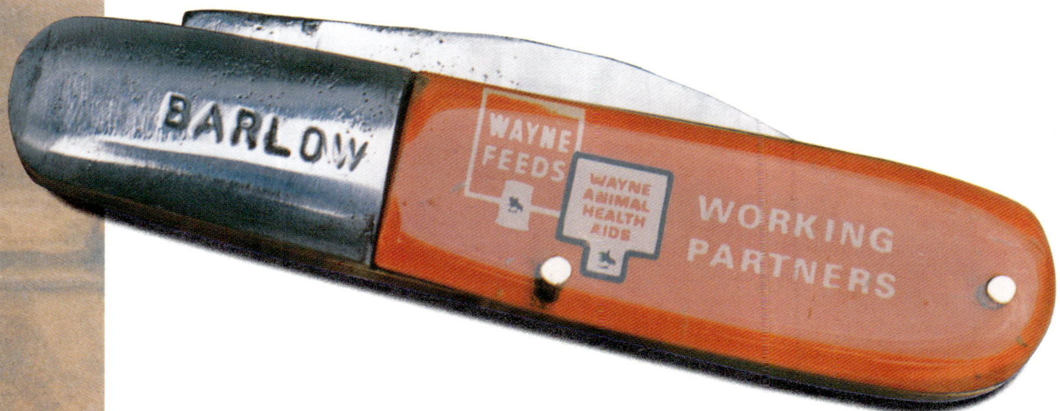

Above: Florist's knives are made with a wide handle for easier holding, and a "sheepfoot" blade for cutting stems. The wide handle provides space for engraving the company name and location, in this case "Roman J. Irwin, New York." This knife was probably given to florists by a commercial growers' association.

Below: The back of the Roman J. Irwin florist knife shows the various products provided by the grower: "Seeds, bulbs, plants and cuttings." Made by the Schrade Cutlery Company, in business from 1904 to 1946. This knife has french ivory celluloid handles, a handle material which has a color uniquely suited for adding engravings. Value is $35–45 in excellent condition.

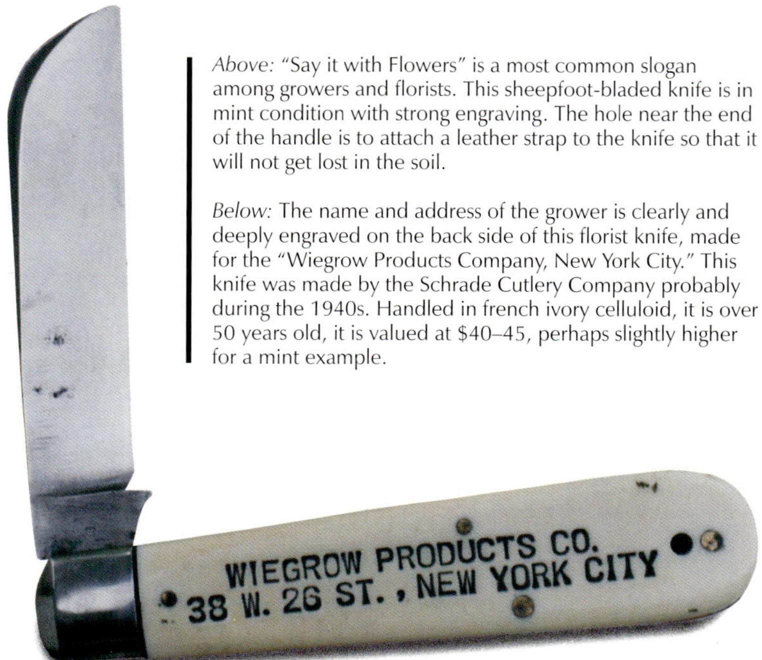

Above: "Say it with Flowers" is a most common slogan among growers and florists. This sheepfoot-bladed knife is in mint condition with strong engraving. The hole near the end of the handle is to attach a leather strap to the knife so that it will not get lost in the soil.

Below: The name and address of the grower is clearly and deeply engraved on the back side of this florist knife, made for the "Wiegrow Products Company, New York City." This knife was made by the Schrade Cutlery Company probably during the 1940s. Handled in french ivory celluloid, it is over 50 years old, it is valued at $40–45, perhaps slightly higher for a mint example.

Although the slogan "Say it with Flowers" is fading over time, this florist knife is an important collectible because it was produced by the Remington Arms Cutlery Company in the 1930s. In this case, the value of the knife is due in large part to the important cutlery name associated with it. Remington is probably the first or second most collected cutlery brand name.

This florist knife was given away by the "American Bulb Company, Chicago-New York." Even though the slogan is fading, the full blades, good snap in the blades and most importantly, the Remington tang stampings would increase the value of this knife to $75–85.

Above left: Although the knife itself is in poor condition, the advertising is very strong. "Vaughan's World's Best Flower Seeds" is deeply etched in the side of the french ivory celluloid handles. This knife would be a valuable addition to any agricultural advertising collection. It value is $30–35.

Sbove right: A typical curved handled florist knife made by Utica Cutlery Company in the 1960s. The famous logo "Say It With Flowers" is deeply etched into the handle material. Although sharpened with use, it still retains good blade snap and length. It has a value of $30–40.

Left: Although the advertisement for "Palmer and Johnson" is beginning to wear off through use, this push blade knife advertises "apple specialists." These knives are useful for slicing apples for tasting, as well as cutting string, opening crates and various other tasks. Generally, these knives are cheaply made, and have a value of $5–10.

Above: Described as a "magician's knife," these small, inexpensively made knives have no "nail nick" from which to open the blade. Instead, the knife operates by holding it upright to allow a small bearing to unlock the blade. Holding the knife in the opposite direction will not allow the knife to be opened. In this way, it opens "magically." This example was a giveaway for Palmer and Johnson, a wholesale fruit and vegetable company in Denver, Colorado. There are some collectors of these magician's knives, which increases the value slightly. The value is $10–15.

Above right: This Barlow was made by the Colonial Cutlery Company, probably in the 1960s. Handled in white plastic, it advertises the "Low Level Dusting Company"—an agricultural crop dusting company out of a small rural town, LaSalle, north of Denver, Colorado. Although its advertising is quite unique, it is of average quality, recent vintage, and its value is therefore $20–25.

Right: The motto for the Low Level Dusting Company speaks loudly of its reputation. "There is no economical substitute for quality" is a lofty goal indeed. Crop dusting is a very unique industry, one filled with not only the hazards of flying, but also those associated with handling extremely dangerous pesticides.

II. FOOD & BEVERAGES

Above: Importing both olives and the final product, olive oil, this knife dates back to the 1920s. Its value lies in the unique advertising, not in its overall condition. Value is $25–30.

Left: This two-bladed metal pen was made by Armser Cutlery Company. Little is known about the "Lion" brand. Lion was perhaps an Italian company which imported both wine and olive oils into the United States.

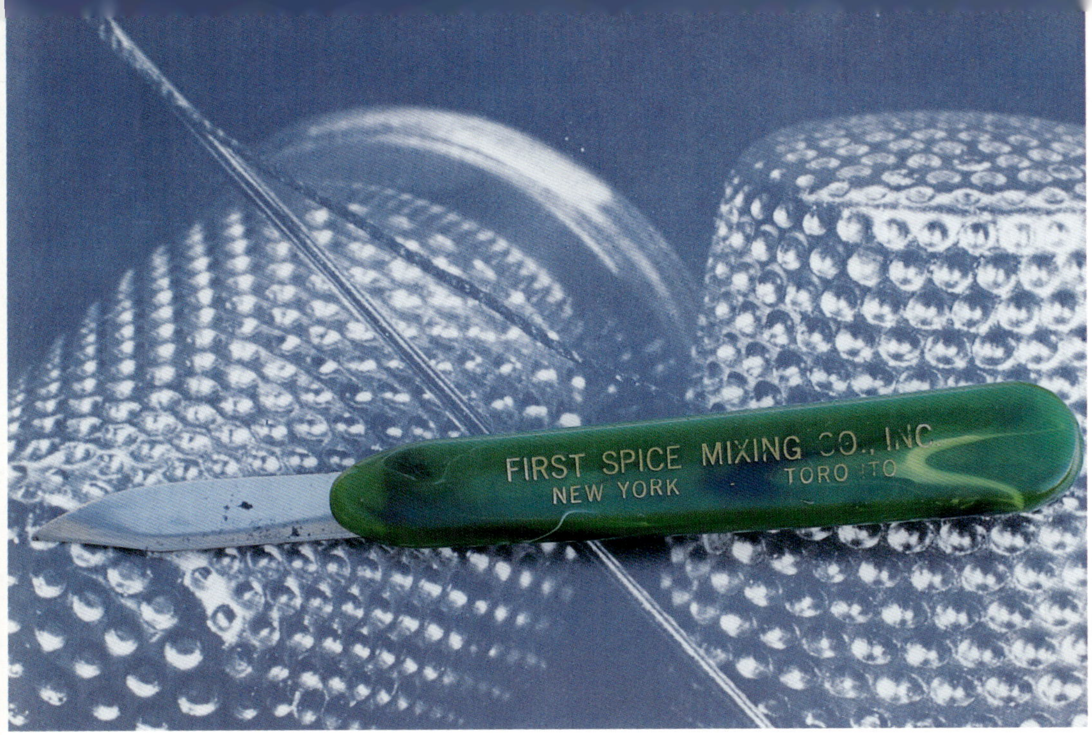

Above left: This advertiser is known as a "push blade," with the blade folding up into the handle. "First Spice Mixing Company, Inc." is the advertising depicted. It may have been given away to housewives, to be used to open packages of flour, sugar, or other spices. Push blade knives are an inexpensive knife but are relatively rare. This one is valued at $10 maximum.

Above right: This "lobster" pattern advertising knife was given to Coca-Cola customers by "BTS," a firm which provided soft drink concessions to major sporting and concert events. Like most other advertising pieces, this knife was given away to promoters, or purchasers of vending products. Designed like a money clip, it is valued at $25.

Left: During the 1940s and 1950s, hundreds of various carbonated beverages were produced from small bottling companies all across the United States. Among the "sun" names used on the sides of colas are the following: Sun Spot, Sunset, Sun Drop, Sun Crest, Sun Ripe, Sunburst, Sunrise, Sun Valley. Although not found in any recent soft drink reference materials, former residents of the Southern United States recognize "Sunbrite" as one of those many colas. Another theory is that Sunbrite was a cleanser or cleaning solution which used the name to advertise what effect this particular product would have on clothing or other cleaned articles. The cutlery stamping used on the tang of the master blade is that used by Camillus Cutlery during the 1940s, known as a "four line" stamping. This knife also contains a unique blade-opening mechanism called the "ring-turn." Because of its age, product advertisement, condition, and ring-turn opening mechanism, this knife is valued in mint condition at $65–75.

Above: This rare and unique knife was made in the late 1970s, by the Krusius Brothers Cutlery in Solingen, Germany. This knife advertises an extremely popular product, Coca-Cola. It is a massive 4-bladed knife with jigged bone handles, in mint, unused condition, with a deeply etched advertisement on the master blade. The knife style would be called a "cattle pattern," or large "cigar pattern." It is valued at $80–85. Even though it is relatively new, it is a very desirable collectible.

Above right: This lobster pattern, metal-handled pocketknife advertises the Coca-Cola Company, which is perhaps the best known advertising company. This knife contains two blades and a fingernail file. Several dozen of these knives in the original wrappers were found in storage, and resold to interested collectors.

Right: A closeup of the Coca-Cola knife shows the German stamping "trink" instead of the American "drink." Made during the 1950s, this knife is stamped Solingen. The value of the knife is $25–35, relatively cheap for original Coca-Cola items. With a large collecting organization, other Coca-Cola knives run as high as $125–150 depending on the age and stamping.

Above left: Leg knives are generally one of the most desirable advertising cutlery collectibles. These, advertising Pepsi-Cola, however, are current reproductions from Novelty Cutlery, Japan. They are an accurate duplication of original leg knives made in the 1930s, complete with slogan. Their value is $10–15.

Above right: The rear of this reproduction Pepsi Cola leg knife is deeply etched with the Pepsi slogan. "Light and Refreshing," the handle proudly proclaims. Unique in design, collectors need to be aware of which knives have been reproduced and which are truly originals. The handle materials of this reproduction are brass. Advertising collectors should take special notice of those leg knives which bear the "Remington" circle stamping. Although Remington did make leg knives in the 1930s (these knives now value at over $150), the Remington tang stamp has been reproduced and passed on as original. Collectors should authenticate any metal-handled leg knives, including the Nehi soft drink advertiser.

Left: This leg knife reproduction is made in China, which is stamped clearly into the back of the master blade. Unlike those made by the Novelty Cutlery Company, Japan, these are not as clear and distinct—there is some blurring of the words. In addition, the fit and finish of the blades and backsprings are more crudely made. As current reproductions, they are worth only $5–7.50.

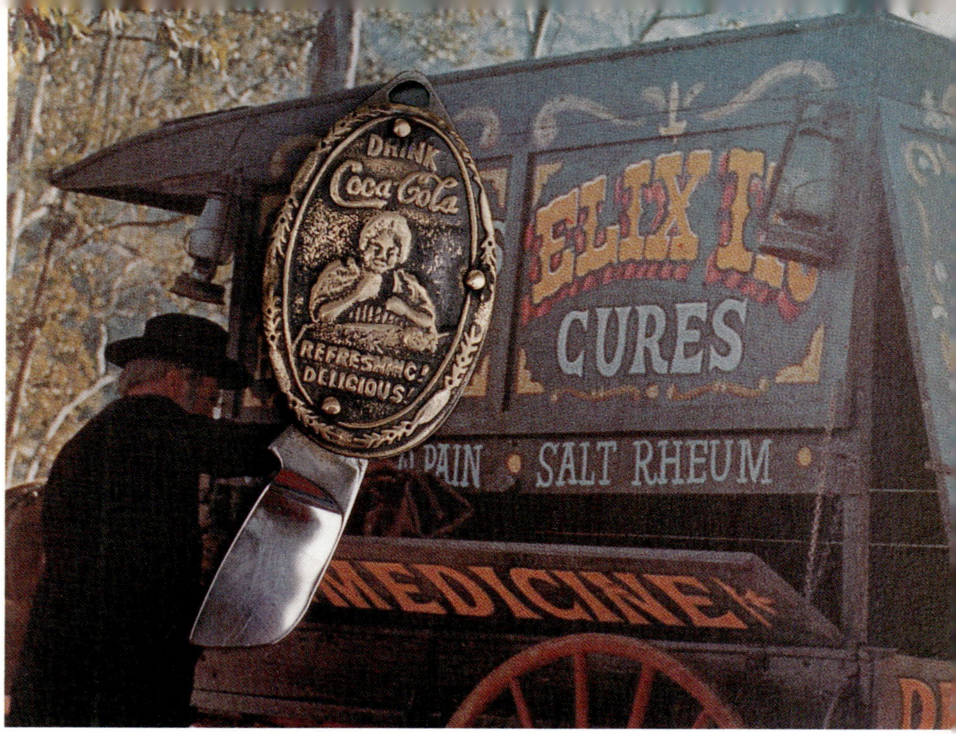

Above left: This leg knife advertises the famous "Nehi" soda pop. This leg knife is a reproduction of one made by Remington in the 1930s. Unlike those leg knife reproductions made in China, this was probably made in Germany, perhaps by the high quality "Fightin' Rooster" Cutlery Company. The slogan on the side states: "Take a look at the bottle, and be sure that it's Nehi." This example is stamped NCCO (Novelty Cutlery Company), but some bear the famous Remington stamping. An original Remington Nehi leg knife is worth at least $150, so perspective buyers of Nehi's stamped "Remington" should have the knife authenticated prior to purchase. This example is worth $30–40, even though it is a reproduction. These were made in the late 1970s.

Above right: Another Coca-Cola reproduction in the form of a dollar knife is made in China. Compared to those produced in Japan, these reproductions are crudely cast, with the actual lettering somewhat blurred. As a novelty, they are interesting, but have little value—$5.

Left: One of the smallest advertisers made, (as shown by the size of the quarter), this knife advertises the Coca-Cola company. The style of the knife is called a "fishtail bowtie" because of the handle end (fish tail) and guard "bowtie." Made by Colonial, probably in the 1970s, it was cheaply made. Value $10, perhaps slightly more to a Coke collector.

This knife was made by Schrade Cutlery Company during the late 1930s to 1940s. Nu-Grape was one of a number of fruit-flavored carbonated drinks to be produced in the United States during this time. Carbonated drinks are important advertising subjects, this one rated at $35–40, perhaps slightly less because of the blade wear. It contains a bottle opener built into the knife handle.

This small "bartender's" style advertiser, with corkscrew and bottle opener made into the blade, for "NuGrape Soda" by the Ambassador Cutlery Company. Ambassador is a relatively common name in inexpensive advertisers, the company starting production in the early 1950s, but soft drink collectibles have always been in demand. The value of this advertiser is $20–25.

Any advertising cutlery piece with the Remington Cutlery tang stamping is rated extremely high. Remington made knives from 1919 to 1940, and this knife was given to grocery store owners who purchased at least one case of Baby Ruth candy. These knives are extremely rare, and are valued at between $100–125, perhaps higher in near-mint condition. This example is handled in jigged black composition.

Baby Ruth candy was named after President Grover Cleveland's eldest daughter, Ruth, by an employee of the Curtis Candy Company. This candy bar was introduced at the Chicago Colombian Exposition in 1893. This closeup photograph of the knife shield shows not only the Baby Ruth name, but the fact that Curtis Candy Company made not only candy but gum as well. These facts make this knife easier to date, and help make it an extremely important collectible.

Above: In addition to producing a serpentine jack knife in black composition, Remington Cutlery made this unique advertiser with brown, jigged bone sides or handles. Bone, as opposed to other materials, is a more desirable handle material for pocketknives. Jigged bone is extremely common on older knives, but is very rare on advertising cutlery. This particular Remington was called a "premium knife," and was given out to grocery store owners who purchased case lots of Curtis candy and gum. Remember, these knives were made between 1920 and 1940 (at the latest), and most likely during the Great Depression of the 1930s. Even major cutlery companies like Remington were going through hard times, and many failed during this time. With the economy almost at a standstill, and money almost nonexistent, it was no wonder that companies turned to premiums, giveaways, and other rewards in order to try to sell their products. Because of the unique stamping, the use of jigged bone, and the very collectible "Remington" tang stamping, this knife is worth $125–150.

Above right: A closeup of the Remington Cutlery "Curtis Baby Ruth Candy" advertiser shows a unique round shield. These knives are extremely rare, and make wonderful additions to every advertising collection, as well as to those who collect Remington Cutlery pocketknives. Although Remington made over a million of this style of pocketknife, for not only the Curtis Candy Company but also Wrigley's Gum, very few have survived. This is truly a premium knife.

Right: This unique advertiser was made by Schrade Cutlery for the "J. L. Kraft Company." The product was "Miracle Whip," and the date of the knife's production is obvious—1937. We think of Miracle Whip as a standard sandwich spread, but its importance lies in its being introduced at the Chicago World's Fair in 1933. It became the largest selling sandwich spread almost immediately. In the middle of the Great Depression, this product gave people something to cheer about. This knife is valued at $45–55, and contains a fingernail file and a bail so that it could be attached to a watch chain.

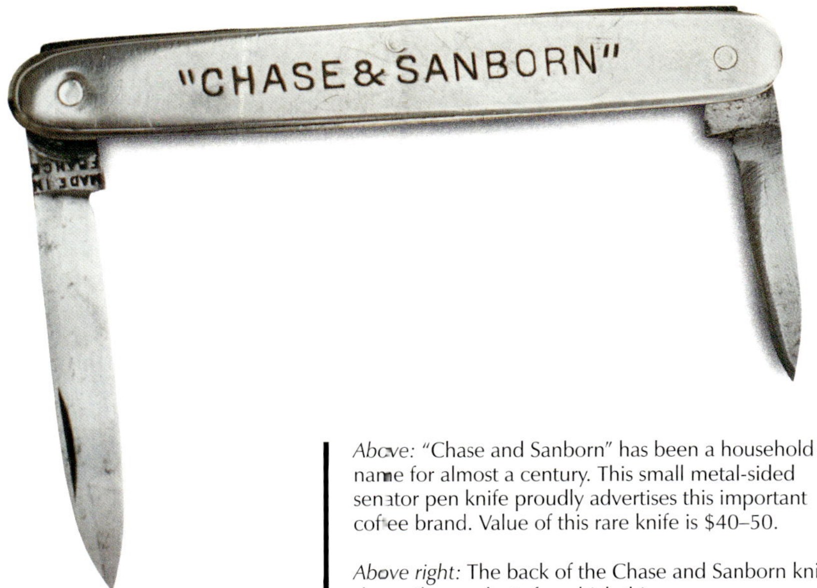

Above: "Chase and Sanborn" has been a household name for almost a century. This small metal-sided senator pen knife proudly advertises this important coffee brand. Value of this rare knife is $40–50.

Above right: The back of the Chase and Sanborn knife shows the products for which this company was once famous for. Since we now know Chase and Sanborn as primarily a coffee company, this knife provides us with some information about its beginnings as both a "tea and coffee" importer. Interestingly, this knife was made in France. One would have assumed that it was produced in the United States, since it advertises an American coffee.

Right: This advertising knife for the "Hutchinson Egg Crate Filler Company," contains a master blade, screwdriver/opener combination, and corkscrew. Made by the Challenge Cutlery Company, of Bridgeport, Connecticut. This knife was produced between 1891 to 1928. Its very good condition, highly collectible tang stamping, and interesting advertising from Kansas make this knife a show stopper. Value is $40–50.

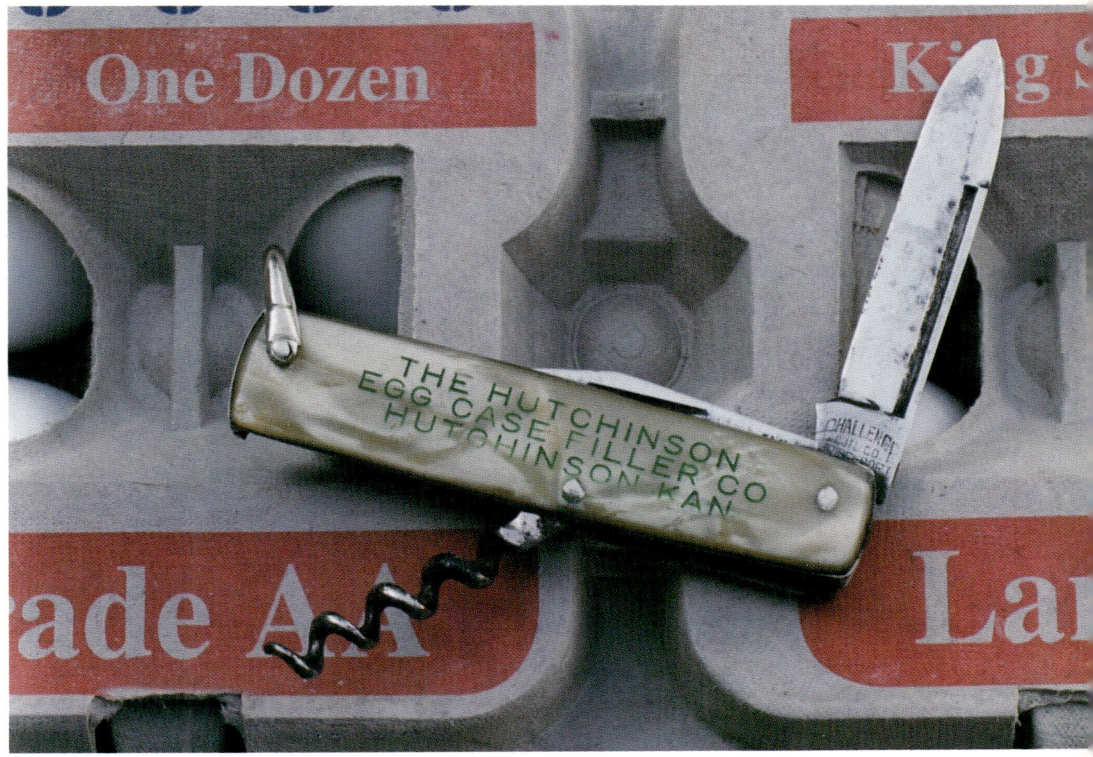

Right: This EZ opener jack made by the Schrade Cutlery Company for "Carey," is called a "wire jack" because, unlike most knives, its handle material is made out of special wire and is not solid. The patent date is listed as 1920, a valuable clue in determining the earliest production date of this knife, although this particular stamping was used into the 1940s. This advertisement proclaims Carey's brand of iodized salt, i.e. "careyized." The Carey Salt Company, like the Hutchinson Egg Crate Company, is headquartered in Hutchinson, Kansas. Value is based on age, condition, and unique style: $30–35.

Below left: "Good Luck Baking Powder" is the advertisement etched on the side of this unique multi-bladed metal knife, called a champagne pattern. Although you would think that it would be given out to housewives who would do the cooking and therefore use baking powder, it was most likely given to chefs and other individuals who were responsible for overseeing the food preparation and kitchens for wealthy landowners. Technically, it is known as a bartender's knife because it contains a corkscrew for opening up champagne or wine bottles, and a blade for cutting the wire found on champagne bottles. This advertiser was made by the Howard Cutlery Company, Germany for importation into the United States about 1880.

Below right: The Good Luck Baking Powder multi-blade with the pen and sheepfoot blade open. The larger sheepfoot blade was used to clip off the end of cigars prior to smoking. In use, the end of the cigar was placed into the hole in the knife. The blade was then depressed to snip off the end of the cigar. These knives are quite rare, and have a value of $80–90 because of the unique design, multi-use function, age, and strong advertising.

Melon Testers

Melon testers are a rather strange-looking pocketknife. Long and slender in shape, they are normally 5 ½" to 5 ¾" in length with a single spear-shaped master blade. Inexpensively made, they contain no bolsters at either end, and are almost always manufactured with "birdseye" rivets at the blade end in order to add additional strength to the knife. In rare cases, melon testers contain a second smaller blade, with the main blade and secondary blade opening at opposite ends of the knife. These knives are also known as citrus knives or sausage knives.

In the cutlery world, where form follows function, melon testers are well-suited for the purpose for which they were designed—inspecting fruit (melons and cantaloupes) or sausages and hams by cutting samples from deep inside of the food product. These knives were originally used primarily by meat and produce inspectors, and it is thought that this particular knife style originated in the 1930s. Before more sophisticated methods of food testing were developed, inspectors used these long, slender knives to cut a core of meat or fruit from the middle of the sample, and proceed to examine it through the senses of smell, taste or touch.

Because the outer skins of many produce and meat products are thick and hard, and serve to protect the delicate insides, the blades of melon testers are often serrated to aid in cutting through this outer skin. Blades are usually made of stainless steel as a sanitary caution.

Melon testers are usually handled in solid celluloid or, more recently, with solid composition materials. White or off-white is by far the most common, with black coming in a distant second. The long sides of melon testers provide the advertiser with a significant "canvas" on which to stencil or etch various advertisements, usually the name of the fruit or meat producer. In addition to the company name,

Above left: Melon testers are the general name given to these large and generally one-bladed knife. These examples show the tremendous variety of advertisements, from individual restaurants to fruit companies, meat producers, and agricultural chemicals, found on the sides of these knives. Because they are infrequently collected, they may be the cutlery advertising sleeper.

Left: Shown with the single blade open, these examples usually contain blades made of stainless steel, a material which resists rusting when exposed to liquids. The etching on melon testers is usually very deep and quite bold, and mint condition knives are still available.

melon testers often contain the company logo or slogan. Like almost all other advertising knives, these knives were designed to be given away to valuable customers, whether it was the local grower, wholesaler, grocer, retailer, or inspector from the Food and Drug Administration.

As a collectible, melon testers have been largely overlooked. They are potentially the last "style" of knife to be collected, possibly because of their awkward size, inexpensive production methods, and the limited number of cutlery companies which produce melon testers. Almost all melon testers are made by the Colonial Cutlery Company of Providence, Rhode Island. As a knife-producing company, Colonial has been in business since 1926; a significant portion of their cutlery production has been melon testers. In addition to Colonial Cutlery Company stampings, some melon testers can be found with Schrade, Ulster, and Imperial stampings. Approximately five percent of all melon testers found by collectors were made by German cutlery companies. These are usually quickly distinguished by nickel silver bolsters at the blade end instead of the characteristic "birdseye" rivets. Most of these do, however, contain examples of various advertisements.

Because it has been largely overlooked by the knife collectors, mint condition examples with deeply etched advertisements can still be found in rather large numbers, at an inexpensive price. Viewed as individual knives, these knives are not very impressive, lacking fancy celluloids, bolsters, or jigged bone sides. Viewed as a total collection of various meat, fruit, or food producing companies, melon testers make a very handsome collection indeed. The future is bright for these very unique cutlery showpieces, with advertising one of the main reasons for their success.

Above right: The names "Swift," "Cudahy," "Wilson Foods," and "John Morrell" are still familiar to shoppers who purchase meats from their local grocery store. These sausage knives were commissioned by these famous meat producing companies. Because it is easier to etch color on white background, the handle material on these knives is usually white, but can be found in other colors.

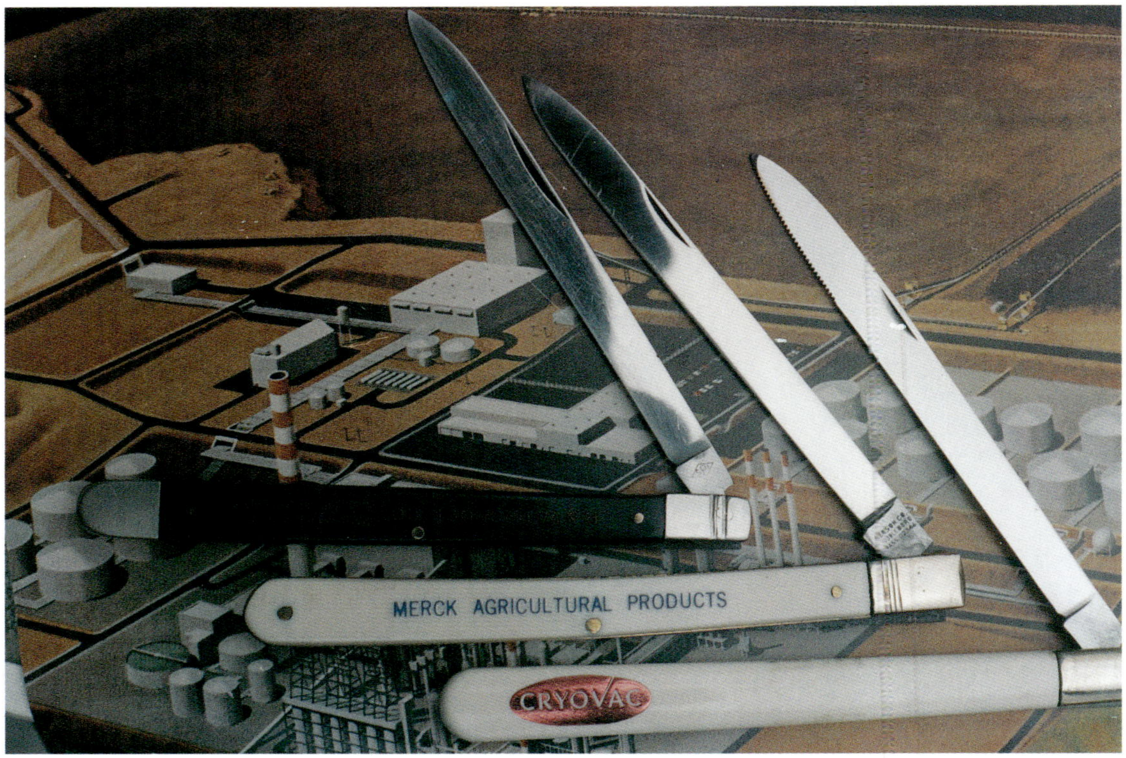

Right: These melon testers are rare in that they all contain a tip "bolster" at the blade end. Knives constructed with nickel silver end bolsters are usually better made, stronger, and fancier. These were all made by German companies.

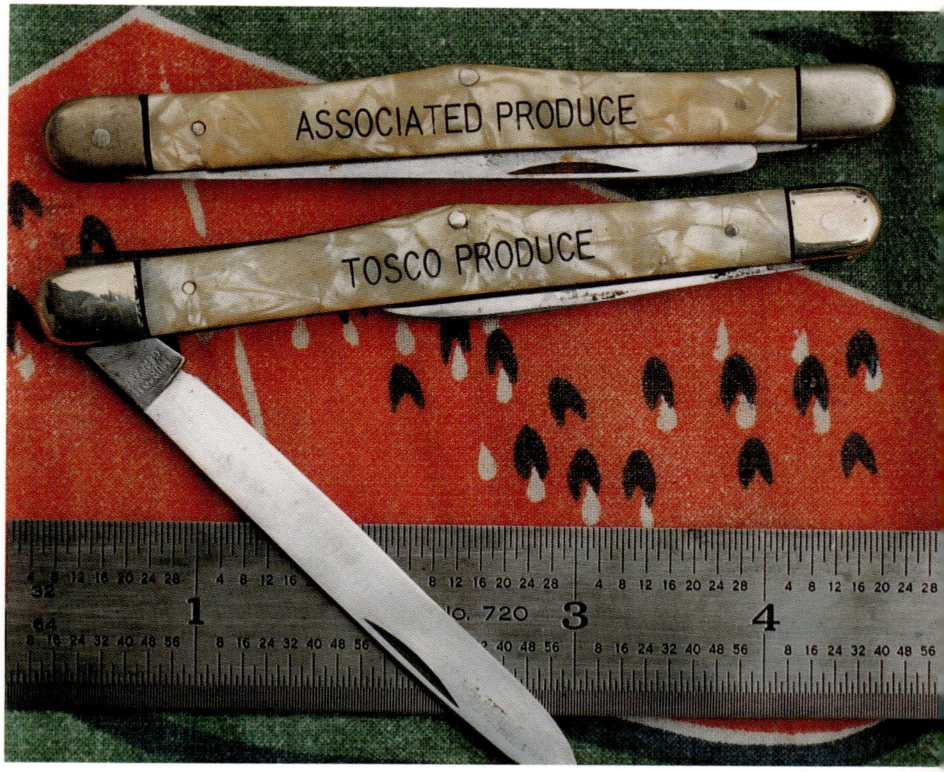

Above left: Mint examples of any advertising knives are always worth picking up. This one for Echrich Products displays their slogan: "From Our House To Yours." This sausage tester, like most, was made by Colonial Knife Company. Because of the strong graphics and mint condition, the value of this knife is $20.

Above right: This pair of unique melon tester advertising knives made for the "Associated Produce Company" and "Tosco Produce Company." They are unique because they each have two blades, and are handled in real cracked-ice celluloid handle material. In addition, they are constructed on a "swell center" style of pocketknife construction. Value of each knife in this group is $25–35.

Left: This mint example of a melon tester is the most common design. Described as a swell end jack, it is one of the largest pocketknives at almost 6 inches. The pineapple company Dole distributed this advertiser to wholesale customers and agricultural product inspectors. Most of these knives were made by the Colonial Knife Company, and most have stainless steel blades for obvious reasons. Value is $20.

Called "sausage knives," or "sausage testers," these knives are very closely related to the melon testers. This example was made by Colonial Knife Company for distribution by "Swift and Company Meats." These knives are generally inexpensively made. A wide variety of melon testers and sausage knives could provide a unique collection. Value is $20.

One of the smallest sausage testers, this one advertises "Armour's Star Summer Sausage." This knife was made by Hibbard, Spencer, and Bartlett, a famous knife company out of Chicago, Illinois. Its age can be dated by the old stamping, the use of french ivory celluloid, and some knowledge of Chicago as the meat packing and stockyard capital of the United States at the turn of the century. In addition, this knife has a small pen blade as a second blade. Value is $40–50 because of its good brand name pedigree, famous product, and small size.

Right: A mint condition full-size sausage tester made by Colonial Knife Company, this black celluloid-handled jack advertises "Dry Sausage," a meat product which can be stored without refrigeration. Birdseye rivets help stabilize the blade, and prevent the blade pin from breaking the celluloid, since these knives have no top metal bolster like most knives. Value is $20 because of handle material, condition and sharp image.

A similar sausage tester made by the Colonial Knife Company for "Cudahy." Made of cream celluloid, this knife is full-sized at six inches. Value is $20.

The "John Morrel Meat Company" gave away this sausage tester to inspectors and wholesale meat buyers. Yellow celluloid was used, and the advertisement includes the formation date of Morrell as 1827, an old American company. Because the engraving is beginning to wear off, the value drops to $10.

The "Wilson Foods Company" had Colonial make this stainless-bladed sausage tester as an advertising giveaway. This mint condition knife make a valuable addition to any collection. Value is $20.

III.

SHOES, CLOTHING, & TEXTILES

Above right: : Many shoe companies used knives as advertising giveaways. Produced by Camillus, and handled in unjigged black celluloid (often called slick black), this example for "Star Brand Shoes" advertises its product within the shield. This knife dates to the 1920s or 1930s, and except for some pitting on the blade, is in very good condition. Value is $40–50.

Right: Metal-handled pen knives are relatively common, but this example from the "Miller Shoes Company, Cincinnati" is unique because the company name and city are imprinted on the same side. Because it is only a one-bladed knife, its value is less than a similar two-bladed variety. The value is $35–45.

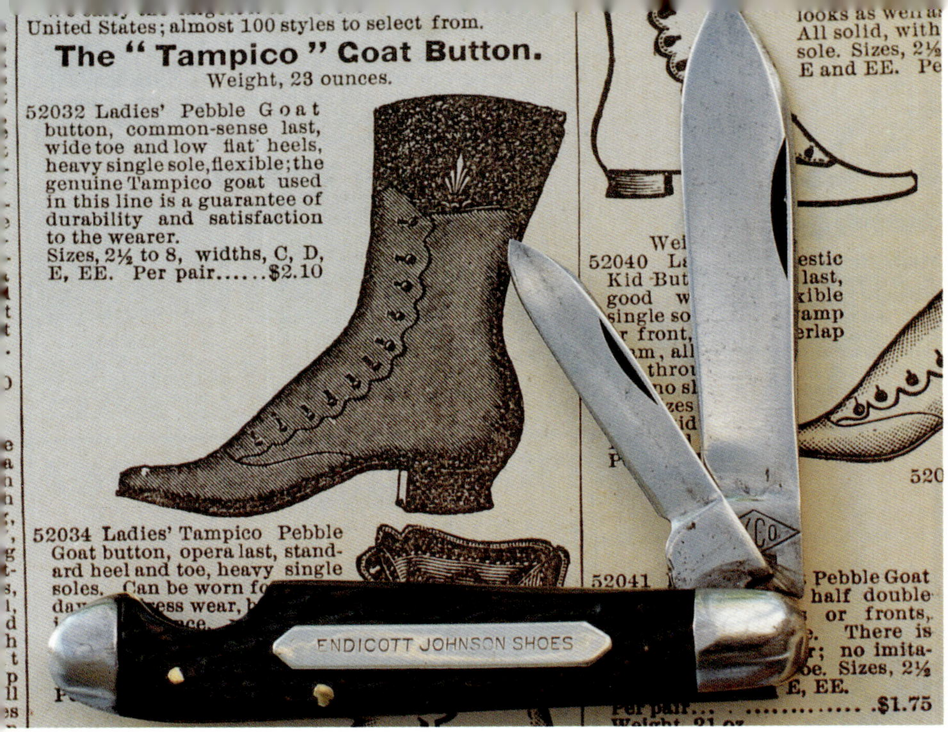

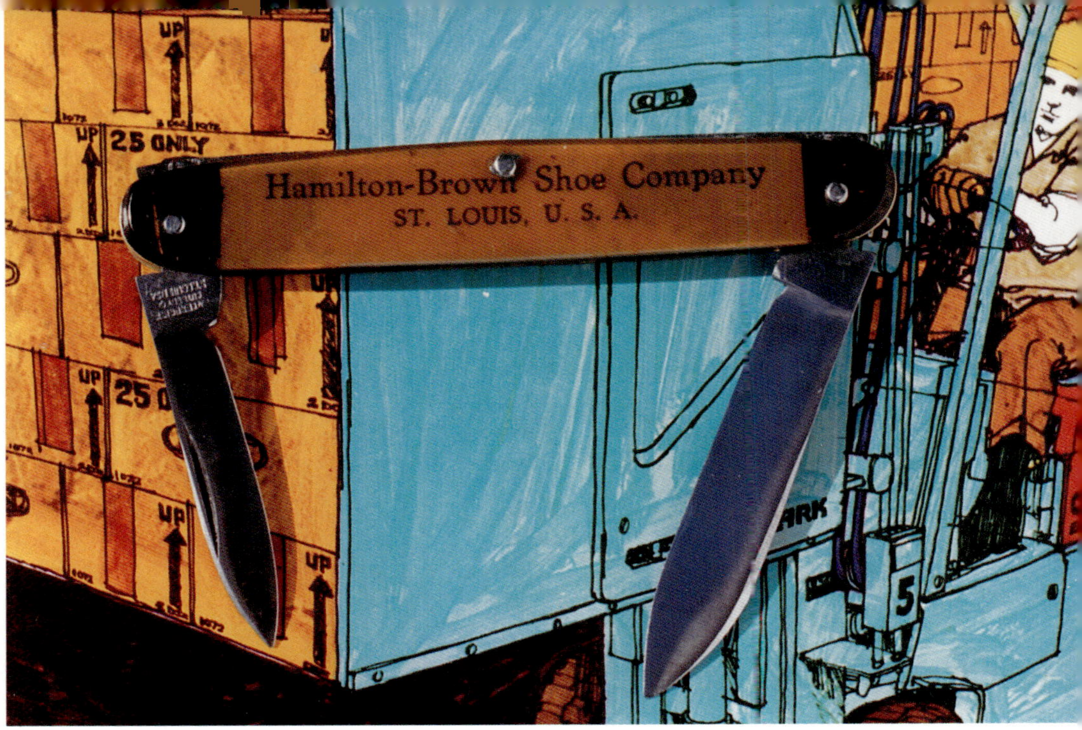

Above: This tang stamping on this "Endicott Johnson Shoe Company" advertising knife reads "IKCO," a stamping used by the Imperial Knife Company during the late 1920s to 1930s. Called an easy (EZ) opener, this knife could be opened by someone without a fingernail by placing the finger and thumb into the notch cut into the knife sides. Shoe knives are an extremely collectible category, and were given to customers who purchased shoes during the 1920s and during the Great Depression in the 1930s. "EZ" openers are rather popular, and this one would have a value of $45–55.

Above right: The "Brown Shoe" advertisements are the most famous of all shoe advertisements. Brown Shoes marketed the "Buster Brown" trademark, which appeared on a wide variety of clothing and food products during the 1920s. This knife advertises the Hamilton Brown Shoe Company, a company which predates the more famous Buster Brown era. This knife was made by the Enterprise Cutlery Company located in St. Louis, Missouri, and was designed to use clear celluloid to cover the company name. Value of this knife is $40, perhaps as much as $50 because of its mint condition.

Right: This "Hamilton-Brown Shoe Company" advertising knife is a metal-handled pen, or a "senator pen" knife. Produced just prior to the Buster Brown Shoe era, this knife is valued at $40–50 because of its metal sides, very good condition, and unique advertising.

Left: Collectors interested in specific dates would find the etching "Makers of Neolin Soled Shoes" stamping on the back side of this Hamilton-Brown Shoe Company knife helpful in establishing the specific date of this knife's production. The date of "neolin" as a material in shoes could be established through trademark research.

Lower left:
This swell end pen knife, with tip bolsters, is handled in yellow cracked-ice celluloid. The oblong shield advertises the "Hamilton-Brown Shoe Company," surrounding the word "quality." The maker of this contract knife is the Utica Cutlery Company, Utica, New York. Utica made knives as early as 1910.

Below right: The rear handle on the Hamilton-Brown advertising knife is inset with a unique shield. It states "Keep The Quality Up." One could easily surmise that this knife was given to shoe salesmen as a reward for outstanding sales or customer service. The value of this knife is $45–55 with the present blade wear.

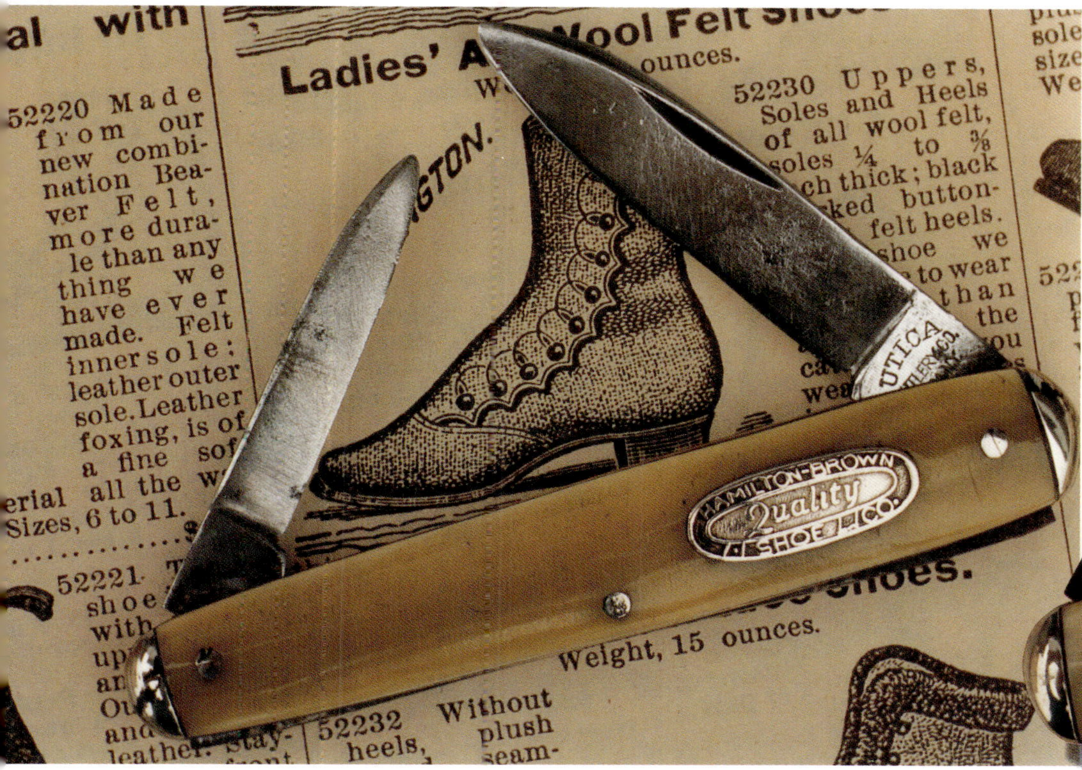

Above: This four-bladed utility knife was the premier "Buster Brown Shoe" advertising knife. Handled in jigged bone, it has a Buster Brown Shoe tang stamping on the master blade. In addition to the master blade, it has a unique spiral leather punch, can opener, and screw driver-cap lifter combination blade. Rare to find in any condition, this knife would be valued at $125–150 in excellent condition.

Above right: A closeup photograph showing the unique "Buster Brown Shoes" shield inlaid into the jigged bone handles of the knife. This knife was probably available to shoe customers by redeeming coupons or stamps received after each shoe purchase. Because it had a punch, cap-lifter, and opener, the four-blade utility knife was very popular with young campers, Boy Scouts, woodsmen, etc.

Right: A second example of the very rare Buster Brown Shoes four-blade utility knife shows the variation in the punch blade. In this example, the punch blade is smooth; as opposed to the circular punch shown in the previous example. Cutlery experts can trace these variations in punch blade styles to various knife companies. This detective work is necessary because the name of the maker of this knife is not stamped into the master blade as in most cases. Instead, this knife bears the "Buster Brown Shoe Company, St. Louis" stamp on the master blade. This knife is also worth $125–150 in near-mint condition.

Below: An "EZ open" jack. This one is handled in jigged black celluloid, and has a very prominent shield which reads "Brown Shoe Company." The strength of this knife is in its historic and famous advertising, not in its worn blades. This knife would be valued at $25–30 because of the condition of the blades. To an individual who collects Brown Shoe Company advertising, it is significantly more valuable.

Far right: A second example of a Brown Shoe Company EZ open jack knife handled in jigged black celluloid. This example was made by the Imperial Knife Company, probably in the 1930s, and is stamped with the "IKCO" tang stamping. This knife has a bail, and bolsters at both ends. It is valued at $35–45 because of its good condition and well-stamped "Brown Shoe Company" shield.

Right: Actual leg knives are by far one of the most valuable of all advertising pieces. Because the two pins through the celluloid are very close to the edge, many shoe knives show cracks in the celluloid. This example is in perfect shape with bright red celluloid, and a clear stamping of "Brownbilt Shoes." These factors along with a full blade makes this an exquisite collectible.

Below: A closeup photograph of the tang stamping clearly shows the Brown Shoe Company, St. Louis stamping on the master blade. Once given away to shoe purchasers who redeemed coupons accumulated by purchasing several pairs of shoes, this knife is worth $125–150 in its present condition.

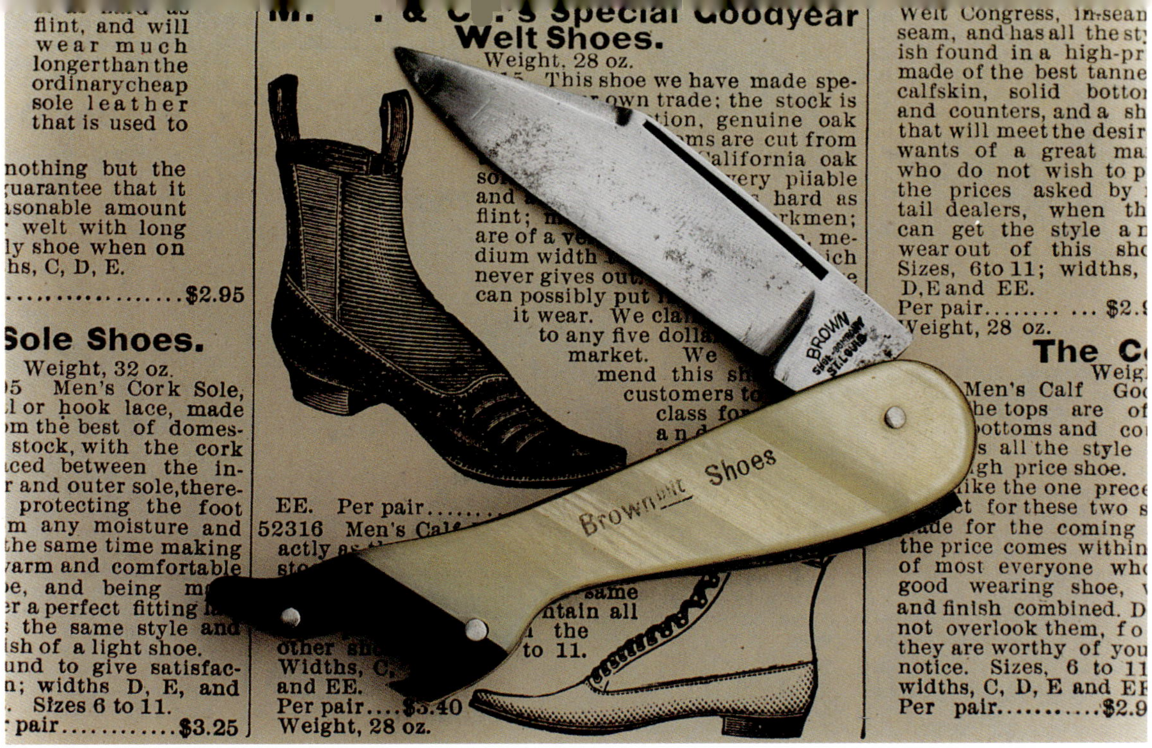

Another rare Brown Shoe Company, St. Louis leg knife. This example uses the rare combination of cracked-ice celluloid and black celluloid to produce an advertising knife which looks like a real shoe. In near-mint condition with original full blades, and no cracks in the celluloid, this knife is worth $150.

This German knife, made with french ivory celluloid, advertises "shoe brushes" with the brand name of "Nugget." Made in Solingen Germany, it is in mint, unused condition. As such, its uniqueness commands a value of $45–55.

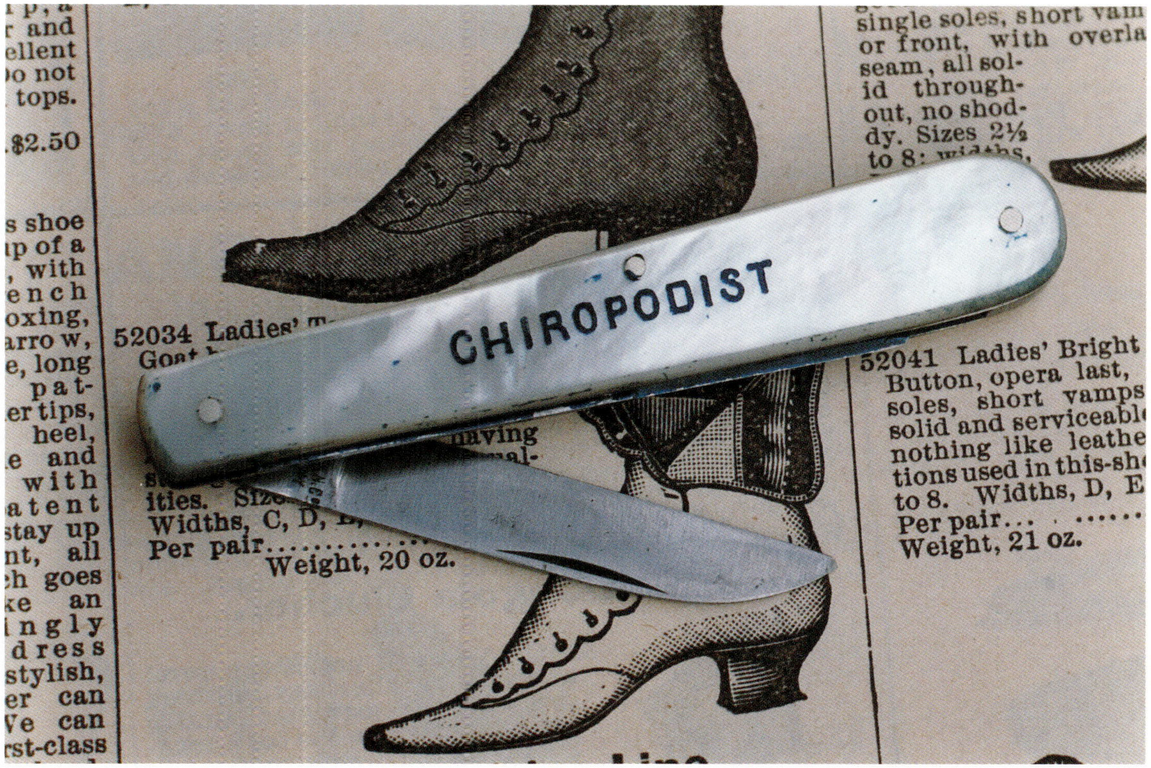

Above left: A unique footwear advertiser with a familiar name. "Poll-Parrot Shoes" was a very famous shoe brand during the early 1950s. Designed for girls and boys, as the shield indicates, this example is handled in french ivory celluloid. This type of celluloid was designed to mimic real ivory, which had a definite grain running through it—this celluloid clearly shows darker stripes running lengthwise through the handle materials.

Above right: The rear of the "Poll Parrot" shoe knife is stamped with the brand name and slogan. "Star Brand Shoes are Better." One of my earliest memories as a child was going to the Poll Parrot shoe store to watch the owner feed the huge parrot he kept in the back of the store. The real parrot was one of the drawing cards to get kids to go with their parents and buy shoes. The value of this knife, with outstanding advertising and fine blade condition, is $50–60.

Left: This unique advertiser is handled in genuine pearl. The name on the side states simply "Chiropodist." In all probability, this was an occupation which is a combination of a chiropractor and a podiatrist—a medical person who could straighten your back or remove corns from your feet. In the early 1900s, tight shoes and bustled waistlines were the rage of the Victorian Age. These tight fittings were designed to give women an "hourglass" figure and small feet. Both of these fashion statements caused damage to the body. Although the maker of this knife is unknown, it is certainly a reminder of the fads and fashions of earlier years. The value is $25–35, perhaps more if the blades were in good condition with maker's stamp. The placement of this photograph along with all of the shoe advertisers would seem natural.

A unique metal-handled advertiser with strong, bold lettering stating the virtues of "Peters Solid Leather Shoes." In mint condition, this advertiser was made by the Richartz Bros. and Sons, LTD, Germany, an old company which made knives as early as the 1930s.

The rear side of the Peters Leather Shoe knife is engraved with the specific brand of shoes made famous by Peters. The caption reads "Peters Weatherbird Shoes." Apparently, these shoes could stand up to all sorts of weather. The value of this 1930s advertiser in mint condition and with strongly engraved slogan is $45–55.

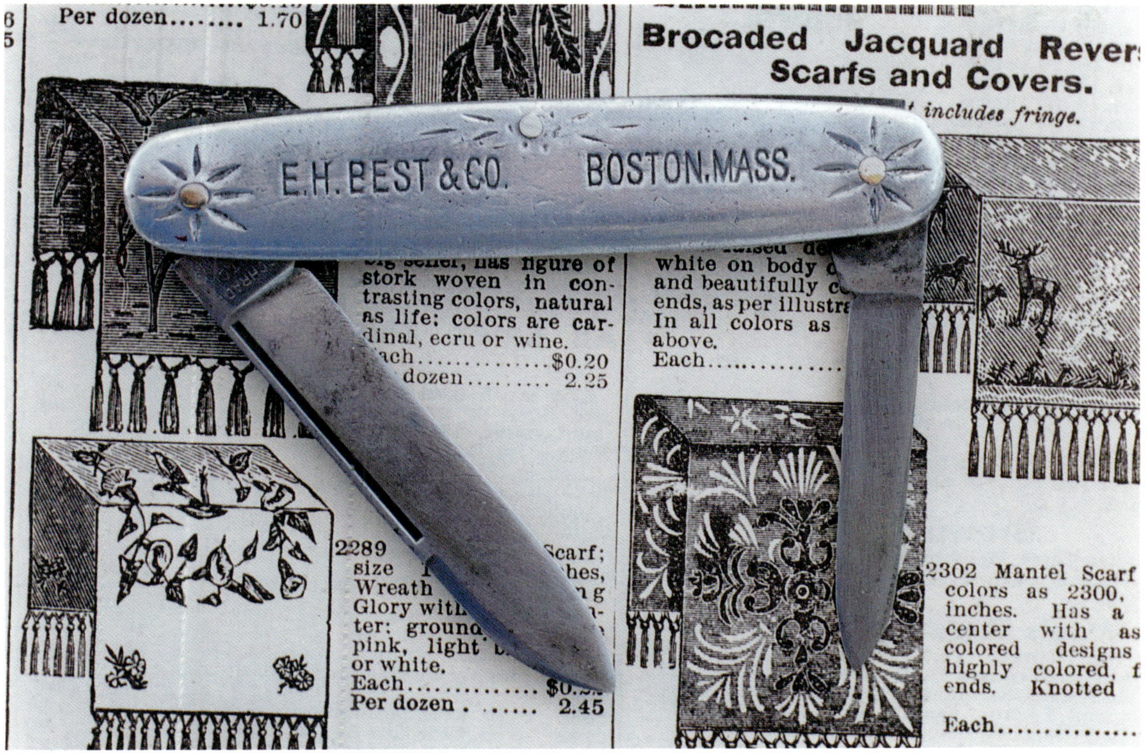

Almost every serious advertising collector has seen, at one time or another, an example of cutlery from the "E. H. Best & Co., Boston, Massachusetts." It is standard fare in every advertising cutlery collection. E. H. Best contracted with several different knife companies to produce this unique advertising pen knife. Search out those examples which have little or no blade wear.

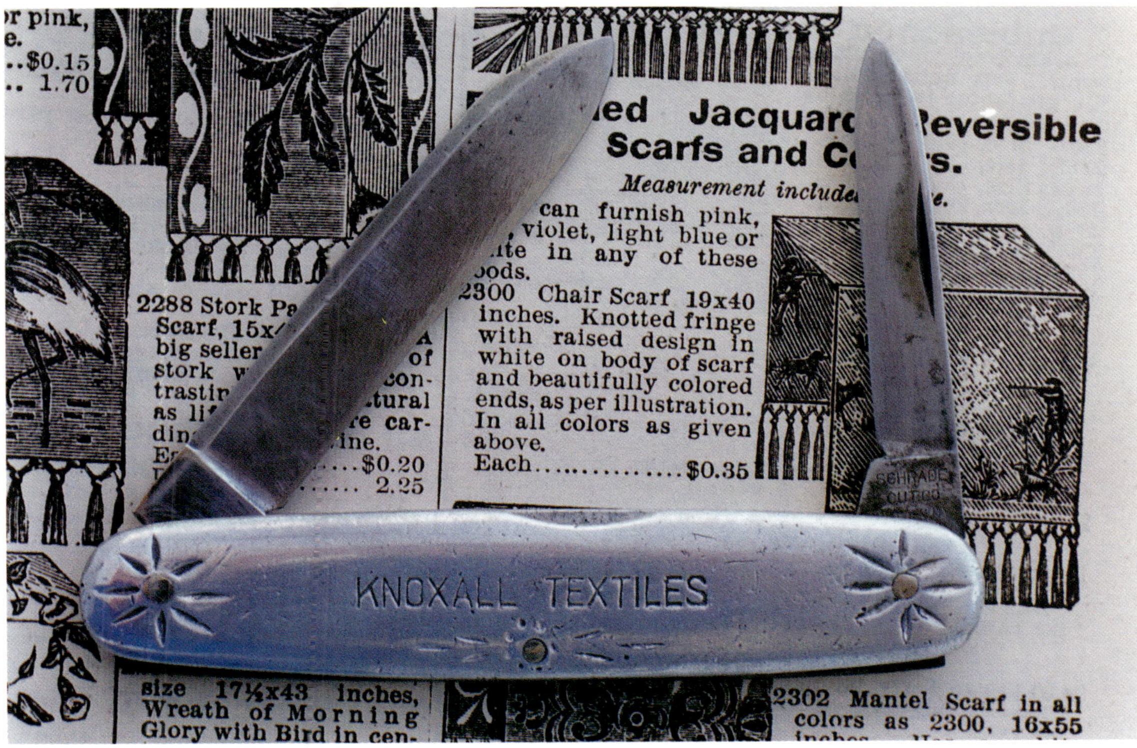

The back side of the E. H. Best & Co. advertiser proclaims one of its major products as "Knoxall Textiles." This advertiser is unique because it is decorated with tooled aluminum handles, seen most prominently around the blade pins on each end, and around the center pin. Made by Schrade Cutlery Company in the 1940s, its condition is near-mint with stained but full blades and great snap. With its Schrade Cutlery stamping and unique design, it has a value of between $45–55.

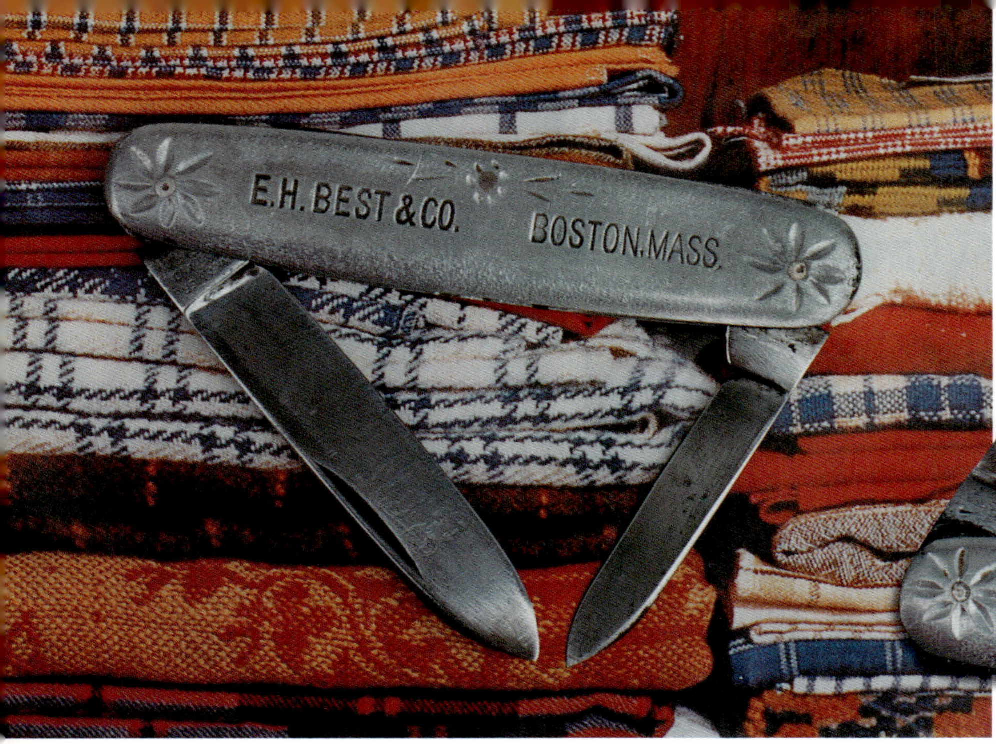

Far left: A second example of the familiar E. H. Best & Co., Boston, Massachusetts advertising knife. This specimen was made by the New York Knife Company—touted as the very best knife company in the United States. Unfortunately, New York Knife Company failed during the first years of the Great Depression in 1931. This fact is invaluable in dating this particular cutlery advertiser.

Left: The rear handle of the E. H. Best & Co. knife advertises "woolens and felts," two of the most popular products produced by this textile company. With sides made of tooled aluminum, and bearing the highly collected New York Knife stamping, this knife is valued at $55–65.

Far left: L. L. Bean is perhaps the most famous outdoor clothing company in the United States, still in full operation. This knife was made on contract by the Western Cutlery Company of Boulder, Colorado in the early 1960s. This knife was found in mint condition with rare yellow celluloid handles. Yellow celluloid is most frequently found on fish knives.

Left: This closeup photo clearly shows the "L. L. Bean Inc., Freeport, Maine" tang stamping on the master blade. Unless this knife was opened, you would never know that is was an important advertising piece. Value of $70–80 is based on mint condition, unique advertising, strong etching, and because its production can be traced to the very collectible Western Cutlery, Boulder, Colorado.

The L. L. Bean name is known to all who appreciate fine clothing. This massive mail-order clothing outlet is located in Freeport, Maine. L. L. Bean contracted this quality advertising knife to the Boker Cutlery Company, Solingen, Germany. The pattern is known to knife collectors as a two-bladed "canoe" pattern, for obvious visual reasons, and was probably offered to customers as an incentive gift. Canoe patterns are quite collectible, especially in the Southern United States. Value of this two-blade with smooth green bone and L. L. Bean etching is $50.

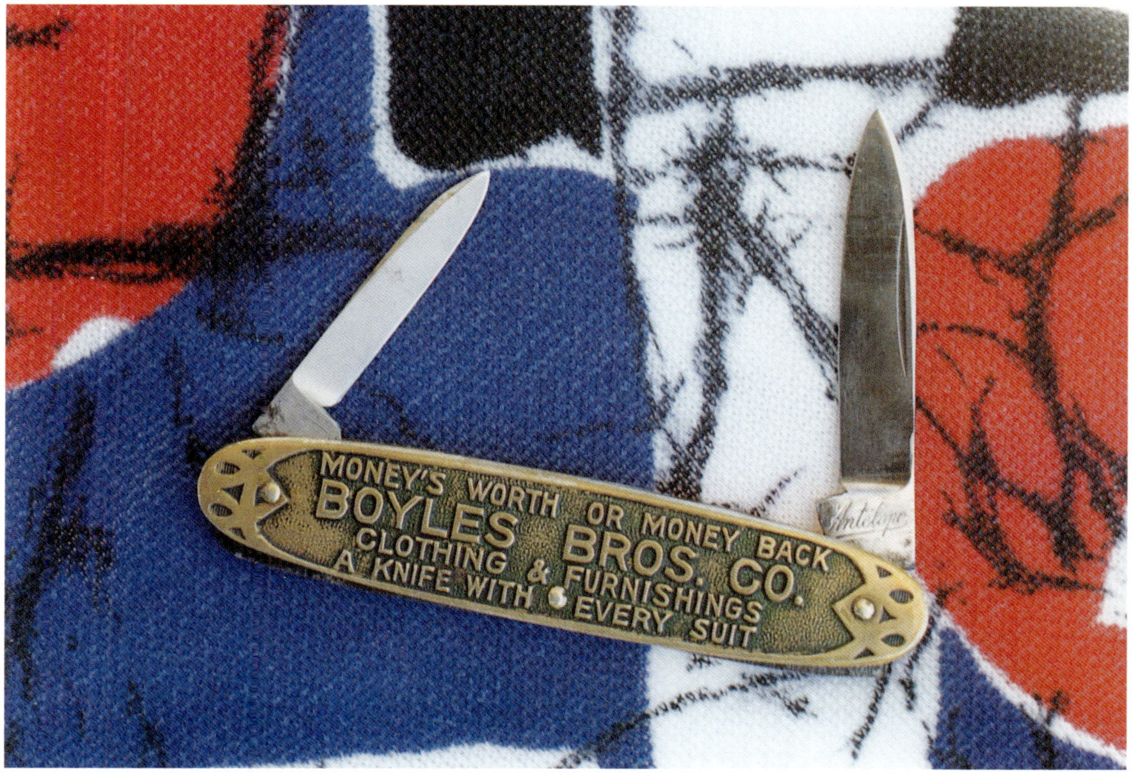

"Boyles Brothers Co." is the strong advertising printed in raised letters on the side of this equal end pen knife. The master blade tang is stamped "Antelope," a German export brand made during the 1930s. This dating information would help substantiate the theory that this knife was issued during the Great Depression in the 1930s. The unique slogan "A Knife With Every Suit," which connects two different consumer products, mint condition, and unique design all make this knife a showpiece of any advertising or cutlery collection. Value is $75–85.

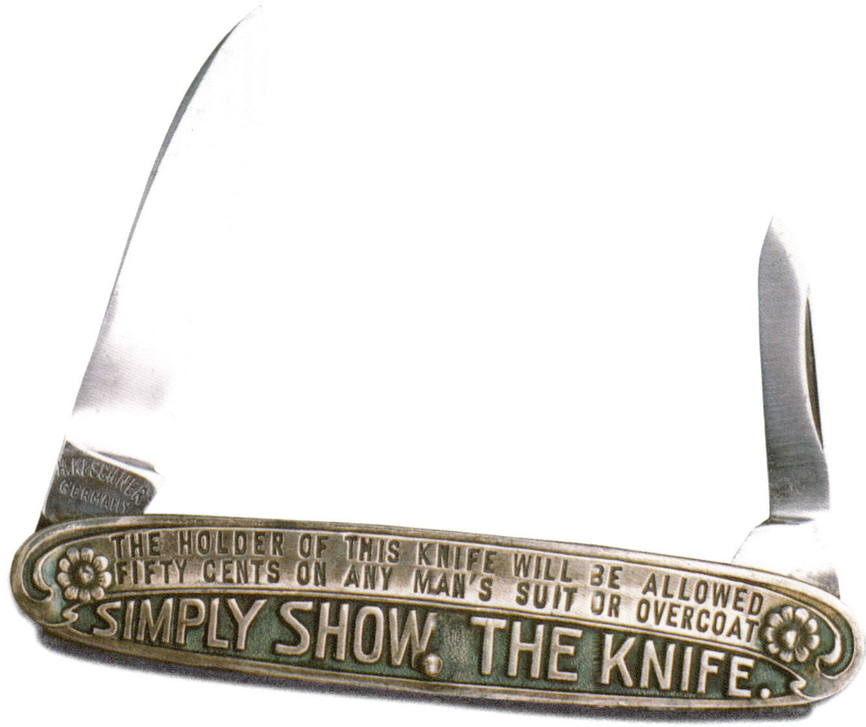

Above left: Rarely do collectors find examples which make up the "centerpieces" of their particular collecting specialty. This example, recently found in Missouri, provides such an example. Imported into the United States by the "A. W. Williams and Company, Newark, New Jersey" in the early 1920s, this knife was made by the A. Kerschner Cutlery Company, Germany. Both sets of names are stamped on the tang portion of the master blade—one on the back and one on the front. The company advertised is "Voigt-Cazeres Company," located in the Nixon Building at 421–6th Avenue, Pittsburg, Pennsylvania. In addition to the company name and complete address, this knife also describes the company with a slogan, "Finest of Clothing Ready to Wear."

Above right: The rear engraved panel of this mint, unsharpened knife tells the unique connection between the advertiser and knives.
In addition to the fancy panels, scrollwork, and flower design surrounding the pins, the engraved lettering on the rear states "The holder of this knife will be allowed fifty cents on any man's suit or overcoat." Then, in bold letters, the knife states: "SIMPLY SHOW THE KNIFE." Just think, fifty cents off on a new suit! Obviously this knife was given out by this clothier to special repeat customers as a sign of appreciation. This is truly the advertising find of the century. Because of its unique slogan, age, strong advertising, engraved panels, mint condition, and rare manufacturer's name, this knife has a value of $85–100, perhaps more.

Left: "Tuf-Nut" is the clothing advertisement imprinted on this "shell-handled" serpentine two-bladed jack knife. Shell-handled knives are cheaply made, with the plastic advertising wrapped around a metal shell. The two sides are then pressed onto the body by clips at each end. As such, they are valuable only for their advertising. Made by the Imperial Knife Company, in the 1960s or early 1970s, this brightly lettered advertiser is in very good condition. It has a value of $10–15.

Above left: Framed against an 1898 Montgomery Ward Catalog, this bone-handled advertiser for "Wards" is in mint condition. Montgomery Ward was one of the first large mail-order companies in the United States. Within the pages of their massive catalogs, isolated customers could find all types of clothing, hardware and fittings not readily accessible in the local towns. It is known that Winchester, the famous gun, knife, and hardware manufacturer, made numerous Wards knives, and that fact adds to the overall value of this particular knife. Winchester shows an identical model in their catalogs.

Above right: Blade etching always adds significantly to the value of any knife, in this case "Master Quality" stamping on the Wards knife indicates a pristine mint knife (sharpening and any moderate use will soon erase this blade etch). Its quality construction, strong tang stamping, mint condition and cutlery advertising, plus the possibility that Winchester made this knife, raises the value to $100–125.

Left: Belonging perhaps to the section dealing with consumer products, this unique advertiser is placed in the clothing and textile section. Its advertisement is very faintly stamped into the metal and reads: "Edward Rose and Company, Tailors, Chicago" Unique about this example is the design of the tailor's six-inch ruler, with attached thread cutter, fingernail file on reverse side, and what appears to be a cigar cutter blade near the pivot end of the foldout knife. In addition, this advertising knife came with an original leather pouch also stamped with the name of the tailors. Extremely unique, perhaps one-of-a-kind, in mint condition, its value would be $65–75, perhaps more.

Above: These keychain advertisers are quite old, probably from the 1950s. The top knife has tip bolsters, and advertises "M. Serman & Co.," and the second knife was a souvenir from "Kansas City, KS.," rare since Kansas City, Kansas is considerably smaller than Kansas City, Missouri.

Right: The rear of the M. Serman and Co. miniature advertiser reads "The Economy Blouse Co." This knife has a rare advertisement, and its value would be $10–15. The Kansas City souvenir knife would be valued at $10–12.

IV. CONSUMER PRODUCTS

One of the most interesting advertising cutlery collectibles advertises "Labreche's Toilet Necessities." This very unique multibladed cutlery piece contains not only a master blade, but also a moustache comb, a combination fingernail file and cuticle cleaner, cap lifter, corkscrew, shoe button hook, and a small celluloid toothbrush hidden in the interior of the knife. Measuring almost four inches in length, this piece is a prized find in any advertising collection.

You can examine the various implements, like the moustache comb and the button hook, for clues to this knife's purpose. The era of its use is clearly stated on the metal sides: "Patented 6, June 1911." Research into the patent date indicates that this was a Canadian patent, as opposed to an American or British patent. An interesting question remains as to the reason for its design and production. Perhaps it was designed to be sold or given to travelers who made long train journeys, or was a utensil made for possible military use. Because of its intriguing interest, unique design, rarity, and outstanding condition, its value is $275–325.

Left: This three-bladed premium stockman advertising knife is handled in genuine stag. The use of stag as a handle material adds greatly to the value, as does the "matchstriker" pull on the master blade. This knife proudly advertises "Pentax" cameras, and was made by the Colonial Cutlery Company. It bears the "Old Cutler" stamping, an older stamping now being revived. Because of its size, stag handles, and premium pattern, it was probably not given away to customers, but may have been especially produced for company executives and given away as a special award. If that is the case, it is quite rare, and rates a higher value. Generally, knives made by Colonial in recent years do not show the quality fit and finish seen in this knife. This knife, however, is valued at $60–75, especially with the unique advertising, and unsharpened mint condition.

Lower left: This advertising knife contains not only a master blade, but also a real blank automobile key. This particular example has never been cut into a key, and the advertisement has never been printed on the sides of the knife. Made by Imperial, this knife is cheaply made, with press-on bolsters and wrap-around celluloid sheets on the sides. Nevertheless, it is certainly an advertising novelty, and was probably given to customers who purchased a car in the 1950s. Value is $15–20.

Below: These lobster pen knives were made for specific companies as advertising giveaways. "Paumier's Insurance" and "Smith Alsop" were the companies which commissioned these knives. Both contain a bail which could attach to a keyring or watch fob. Since brand recognition is always important in any advertising collectible, generally unknown companies are priced lower than nationally known products. These were made by Imperial Cutlery Company, and are valued at $10–18 each, depending on condition.

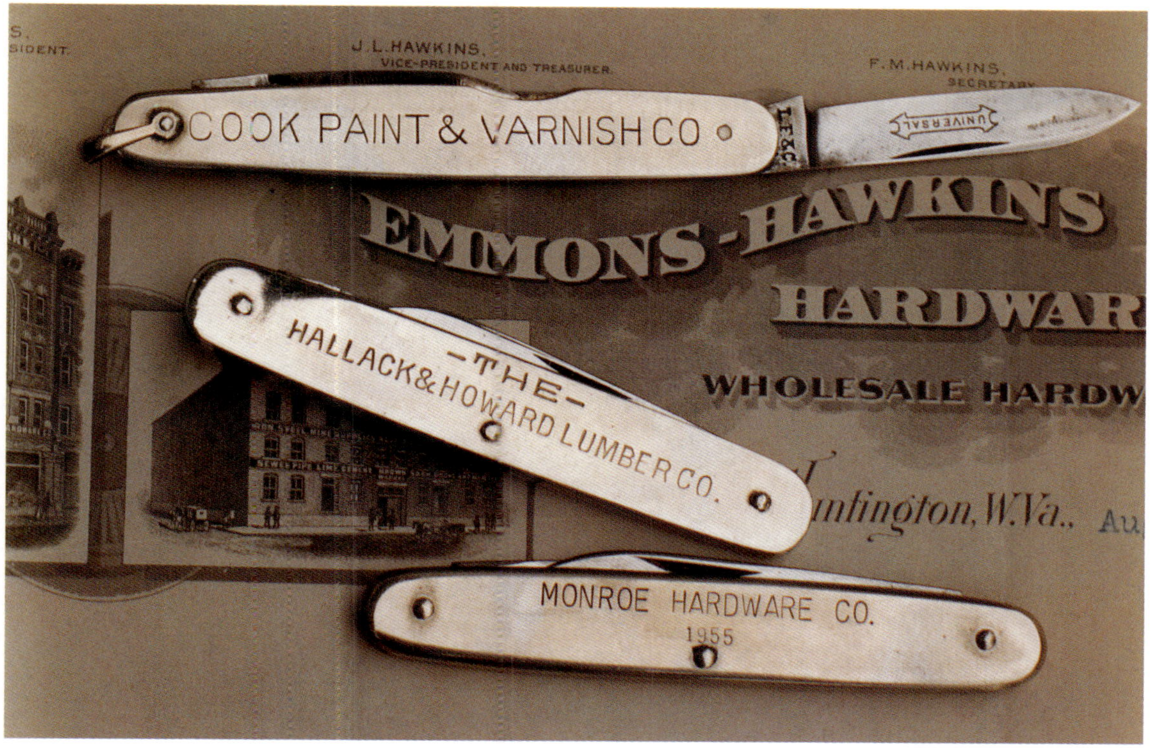

Above left: This jigged, bone-handled two-blade is an extremely unique cutlery conversation piece. Its two identical blades sport fine "tooth-like" striations with sharpened edges. It is classified as a "dog comb"; its sharpened projections were used to comb out the hair on small, wire-haired terriers, trimming the matted hair in the process. There was a time when these small feisty terriers were used to hunt and rout out burrowing rodents and hares hiding in the undergrowth in Great Britain. The dogs emerged from these hunting trips with dirty, matted hair, full of brambles and stickers. The only utensil which could successfully manage this matted hair was the dog comb.

Above right: A closeup of the tang stamping on this jigged bone-handled dog comb reveals lots about this advertising piece. "Spratts" is the name of a British dog food company; this knife was probably given away to valued customers upon purchase of quantities of dog food. The Spratt's stamping is approximately 1912, which truly makes this mint knife an advertising cutlery find. It is valued at $95–110 in this condition.

Left: An interesting collection of advertisers could be put together built around a specific theme—in this case, metal-handled advertisers given out by hardware and lumber companies. These knives might be combined with other advertising pieces from the same industries. By selecting a specific theme, collectors have some focus from which to build a collection.

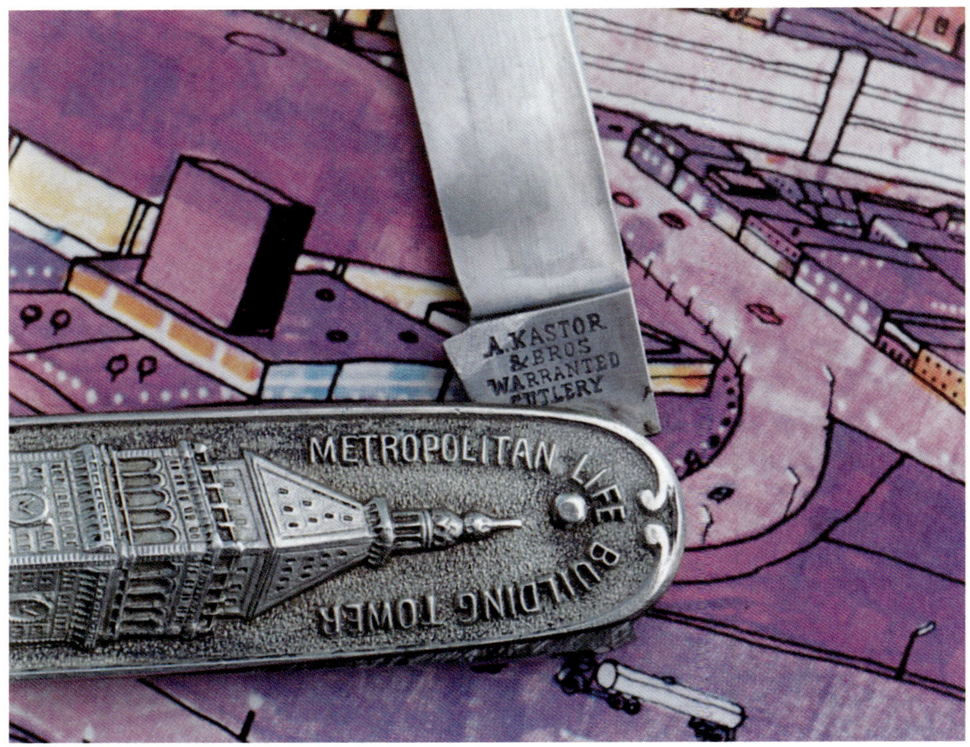

Above: This knife is one of the premier advertising knives ever to be found. It has the unique raised lettering, metal sides and fancy end scrollwork of a show stopper. Given away by the New York office of the "Metropolitan Life Insurance Company," it is in perfect condition. This knife represents "pristine mint" condition—unsharpened, unused, and showing no signs of wear.

Above right: The "Metropolitan Life Insurance" knife is even more unique when turned over to the rear side. The metal rear side is embossed with a raised miniature skyscraper surrounded by two important facts about the building. The words "Tallest Building in the World" appear on the bottom of the knife, and "Metropolitan Life Insurance Building" encircles the building's tower.

Right: This extreme closeup of the Metropolitan Life Insurance Building knife clearly shows the tang stamping etched into the master blade. Marked "A. Kastor & Bros.," a German cutlery company, this knife dates from the late 1890s. Value of this knife, because of its historical interest and pristine mint condition is $100–150.

Cutley Piece Advertises "World's Tallest Building"

Although metal-sided advertising pocketknives are gaining rapidly in popularity among collectors, the most coveted examples are those which have special embossing on the metal sides. Add special figures or designs and you have a real advertising treasure.

The unique advertising pocketknife commissioned by the Metropolitan Life Insurance Company of New York around the turn of the century provides a special example of this type of advertising treasure. The company's building is carefully reproduced in embossed metal along the front side of this unique metal advertising pocketknife. This building was produced at the beginning of the "skyscraper era," which lasted from approximately 1880 to 1900. During this time of frantic building and architectural "one-upmanship," skyscrapers were sprouting up like weeds on the island of Manhattan.

Before this era, the height of skyscrapers was generally limited by the overall weight of the masonry structures, and rarely reached above ten stories in height. During the period known as the "functional" period, around the turn of the century, new methods were devised in which lightweight steel structures were used as a skeleton to support much lighter facades of stone or terra cotta, with the addition of larger areas of glass windows. With these new design and construction methods in place, architects could build skyscrapers which would escape the traditional constraints of structural weight.

When the plans for the Metropolitan Life Insurance Building (called the "Met") were revealed, some skeptics complained that the bell tower looked surprisingly like the famous *Campanile* in St. Mark's Square in Venice, Italy. Although the architect denied that such "plagiarism" had taken place, several officials continued to lodge complaints against the architectural firm which had developed the building plans. In spite of these complaints, the Met Building was completed in 1909. Reaching a height of 700 feet, the Metropolitan Life Insurance Company could claim to have built the "World's Largest Building."

This claim, however, was short-lived; the famous F. W. Woolworth's Building was built a short time later. Woolworth's was completed in 1913, reaching a height of 792 feet. The Met Building was the world's tallest building for only 4 years, from 1909-1913. As a comparison to later buildings, New York's Chrysler Building was completed in 1930, at a height of 1046 feet, and the Empire State Building completed in 1931 at 1250 feet. More recent comparisons include the John Hancock Center in Chicago, completed in 1969 at a height of 1127 feet, and the Sears Tower in Chicago, completed in 1974 at the height of 1454 feet. The Sears Tower is over twice as tall as the Metropolitan Life Insurance Building.

For advertising cutlery collectors, these facts make this knife an exciting find and makes for interesting research. Rarely does a knife collector have the opportunity to trace the actual production of a knife to only a four-year span. The stamping on this knife gives us some additional information about its production dates. The tang stamping reads "A. Kastor and Bros. Warranted Cutlery." The backside of the master blade is simply stamped "Germany."

A. (Adolph) Kastor and Bros. was a German company which began operating in the United States in 1875. In 1902, they purchased the famous Camillus Cutlery Company of Camillus, New York, and began making knives with the familiar Camillus Cutlery stamping on the master blade. In addition, Camillus began making knives on consignment for various hardware companies, stamping these knives with a variety of hardware store names as requested. Even though Kastor purchased the cutlery factory in 1902, and had production facilities to produce thousands of knives, they continued to make knives in Germany and import them into the United States. This seems to be what happened to this Metropolitan Life Insurance metal advertising knife. The theory is substantiated by the "Germany" stamping on the back of the master blade.

Because of changing U. S. sentiment toward German imported products, the United States Congress passed several very strict laws imposing severe tariffs against German imports. In order to expand the United States market and avoid these devastating tariffs, Kastor, a young hardware and cutlery importer, purchased the New York company. By purchasing Camillus, he could continue to market razors and cutlery products in the United States.

Above left: "The Capital Life Insurance Company, Denver Colorado" is the advertisement engraved on the side of this metal equal end pen made by the Griffon Cutlery Company. Griffon has been in business since the turn of the century and is quite collectible in its own right. In addition, metal-sided advertising knives are presently in demand, and this example would be a valuable find. Although its stamping is a little light, its value is $40–45 in its near-mint condition.

Above right: This old advertiser is unique because of the company name—"Franklin Fire Insurance Company." Very few fire insurance companies still exist; most are known just as insurance companies. This unique lettering helps date this knife between 1900–1920s. The location of the Franklin Insurance Company is indicated on the front as Philadelphia. This lobster pattern knife with scissors is valued at $40–45.

Left: Lobster pattern knives are common styles to bear advertising. This example, advertising the "Home Insurance Company, New York," is quite old, and was produced by the firm of J. E. Mercott, Newark, New Jersey, probably around the turn of the century. Notice that this advertiser does not say "life insurance," a common notation, but only the word "insurance." It is unique because its metal sides resemble a peanut with their indentations. Its outstanding shape, unique advertising and full blades (plus scissors) would add to its value of $50–55.

Left: Mint advertising knives are always sure to appreciate in value at a faster rate than those with worn blades. This example is from the world famous "Travelers Insurance Company," located in Hartford, Connecticut. Hartford is known as the "insurance capital of the world." This example is interesting because it was given out by the "ticket department." This unusual wording might indicate that Traveler's issued not only insurance, but also tickets to various destinations. Made by L.F. & C.(Landers, Frary and Clark), located in New Britian, Connecticut, it was probably made in the late 1930s. As a mint metal-handled advertiser with interesting engraving and famous advertisement, it is worth $50–60.

Below left: Company names with product names on the same side are more valuable than ordinary advertisers, as this "S. C. Johnson's Wax" knife illustrates. This is a "corn knife," used around the turn of the century to literally shave corns and callouses off of the feet of women who wore too-tight (but apparently stylish) shoes. Corn knives are an interesting group of collectibles, made with extremely high-tempered blades which hold a true razor's edge. Why this particular corn knife advertises Johnson's Wax is a mystery. Presumably, it was women who needed the services of a corn knife, and also did the waxing around the home.

Below: The back of the S. C. Johnson's corn knife shows the particular product being advertised—"Johnson's Floor Wax." This example is of very high quality, made by the Jacoby & Wester Company. It dates prior to 1915. Notice the uniquely shaped blade. A very old and unique celluloid-handled advertiser, its value is $40–50.

Above left: Rarely are advertising knives made in the 4-bladed scout or utility pattern like this one for the "Edwin F. Guth Company," located in St. Louis, Missouri. This knife was made by Imperial Knife Company in the 1920s or very early 1930s, and is handled in yellow cracked-ice celluloid. Because of its condition, its value is $45–50.

Above right: The two products highlighted on the back of the Edwin F. Guth advertiser are "Excelux" and "Optilux." My research failed to turn up what specific product was being advertised. Perhaps eyewear (optic), or maybe pharmaceuticals.

Right: Singer Sewing Machines are perhaps one of the most recognized trademarks in American industry. For this reason, this small metal-handled knife has particular significance. Interestingly, however, this knife was made by the John Watts Cutlery Company in Sheffield, England. This English company started making cutlery before the turn of the century. The value of this advertising piece, because of somewhat worn blades, is $40–45.

Above left: This multibladed advertising knife for the Ford Motor Company is a copy of the famous Victorinox models with red handles. It is of very recent production, probably made during the 1980s. Automobile advertising knives are fairly common, with those made during the early 1940s and 1950s (or earlier) commanding premium prices. This model has a value of $10 in mint condition.

Above right: This small Chevrolet advertising piece is a modified lobster pattern, actually with a small ink pad inside of the hollow center. Given to customers or salesmen, it is an interesting piece. Because of the unusual ink pad enclosed, the value is $15–22.

Left: This unique advertising knife was made for the mechanic and repairman to work on both radios and autos. Handled in rough or jigged black celluloid, it contained two blades, the master blade and a second blade which was both cap lifter and screwdriver. In excellent condition it is worth $65. This example, however, is only in fair to good condition because of the wear on the master blade. Its value is closer to $30.

Right: This beautifully enameled advertiser for "Cutter Animal Health Laboratories" is known as a "Toledo Scale" style. It contains not only a large master blade, but also a fingernail file and smaller pen blade. This German made knife was made by J. Bierhoff, Solingen Germany, circa 1920s and 1930s, but research indicates that it was most often sold in Holland. "Toledo Scale" knives are characterized by intricate wire designs over black backgrounds, and are a premium-made knife. Because of its intricate design, outstanding mint condition, and age, its value is $55–65.

Below left: A second version of a beautiful advertiser made by J. Bierhoff, Solingen Germany was found advertising another animal health product, in this case "Chemagro Corporation, Animal Health Division." Looking almost exactly like the Cutter Animal Health Laboratories design, it contains a master blade and pen blade offsetting each other, and a long fingernail file on the opposite side.

Below right: The rear of the Chemagro Corporation advertiser shows the beautiful "Toledo Scale" style of engraving and filling with color, in this case, a red color. In mint condition, as this example is, its value is $55–65. Together, these advertisers make an outstanding pair.

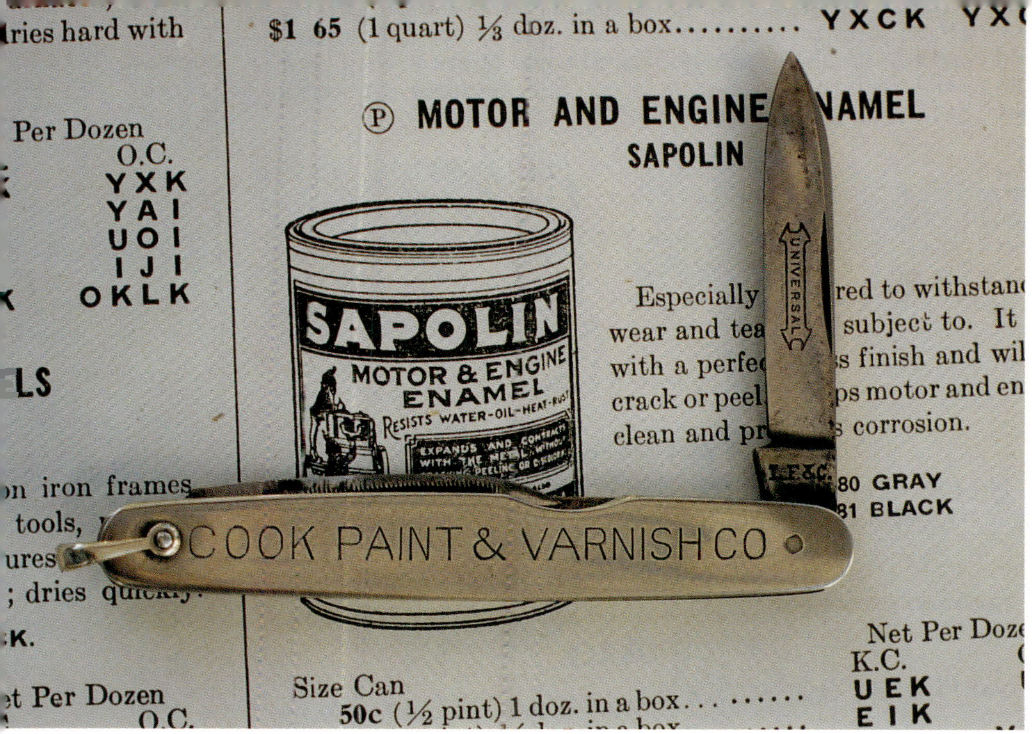

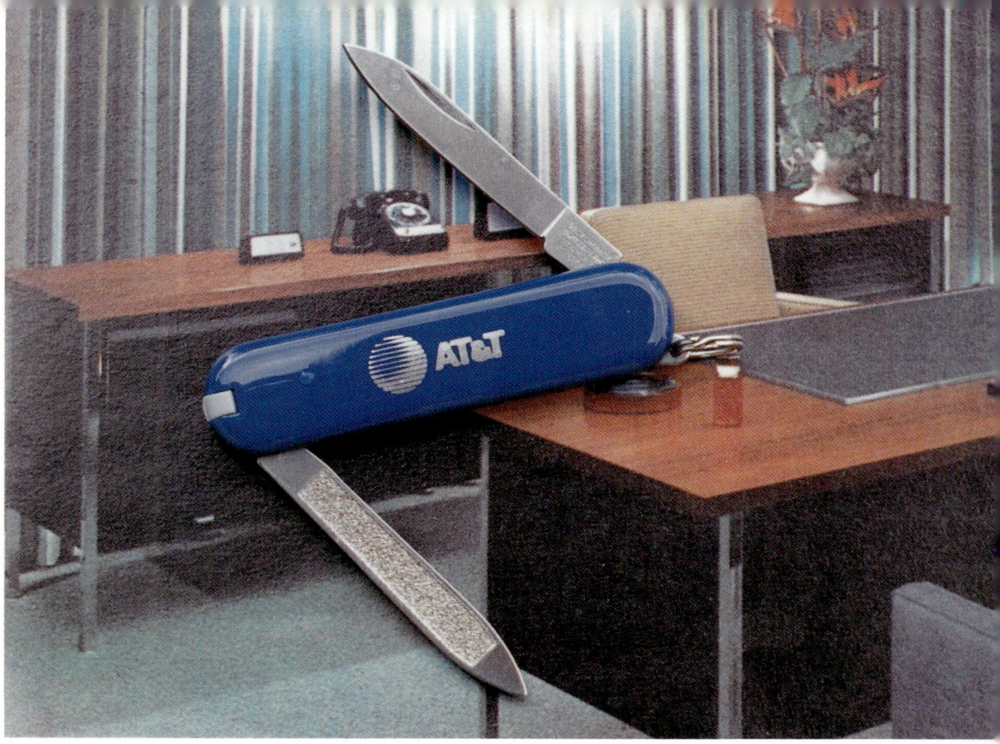

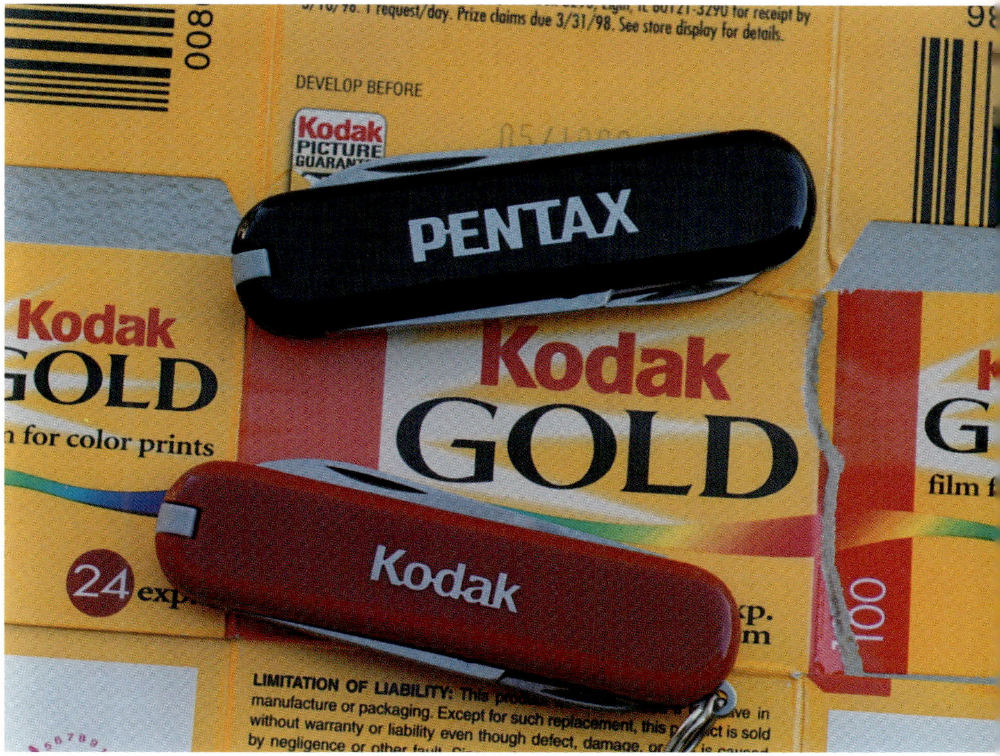

Above: Landers, Frary and Clark, (L. F. & C. logo) located in New Britain, Connecticut, was the producer of this advertising knife for "Cook Paint and Varnish Company." This knife was probably given out to customers or contractors who purchased quantities of paint and supplies. The metal-sided, two-bladed senator pen is etched not only with the advertisement, but the master blade is etched with L. F. & C.'s slogan, "Universal." Its value, because of the condition and outstanding advertising, is $45–55. The bail attached to the end of the knife indicates that this knife was intended to be hung on a watch fob chain.

Above right: Victorinox was the producer of the knife engraved with the household name "AT&T" (American Telephone and Telegraph). Like other small Victorinox knives, these were probably given to customers who had accounts with AT&T. Value is $10–20 each.

Right: These small authentic Victorinox knives are designed to fit on key rings or in purses. These were etched by Victorinox for "Pentax" (cameras) and "Kodak" (film). Each contains a master blade, fingernail file, scissors, toothpick, and tweezers. Examples like these could be collected for a very inexpensive price and a unique collection could be put together. Value $10–20, depending on advertising.

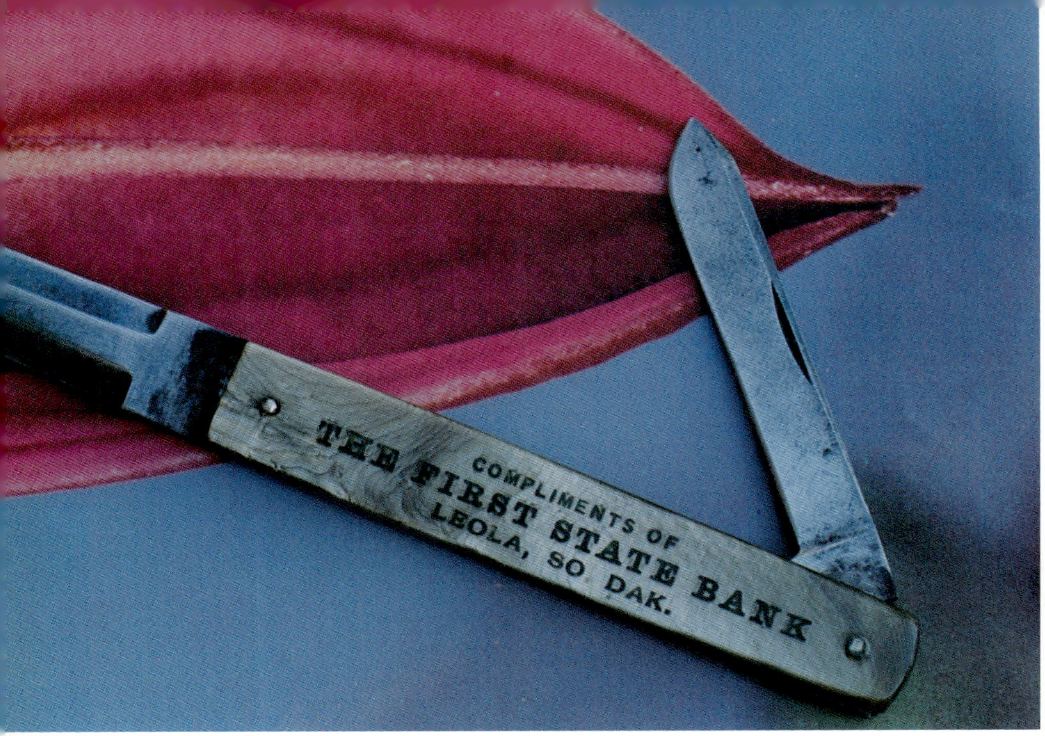

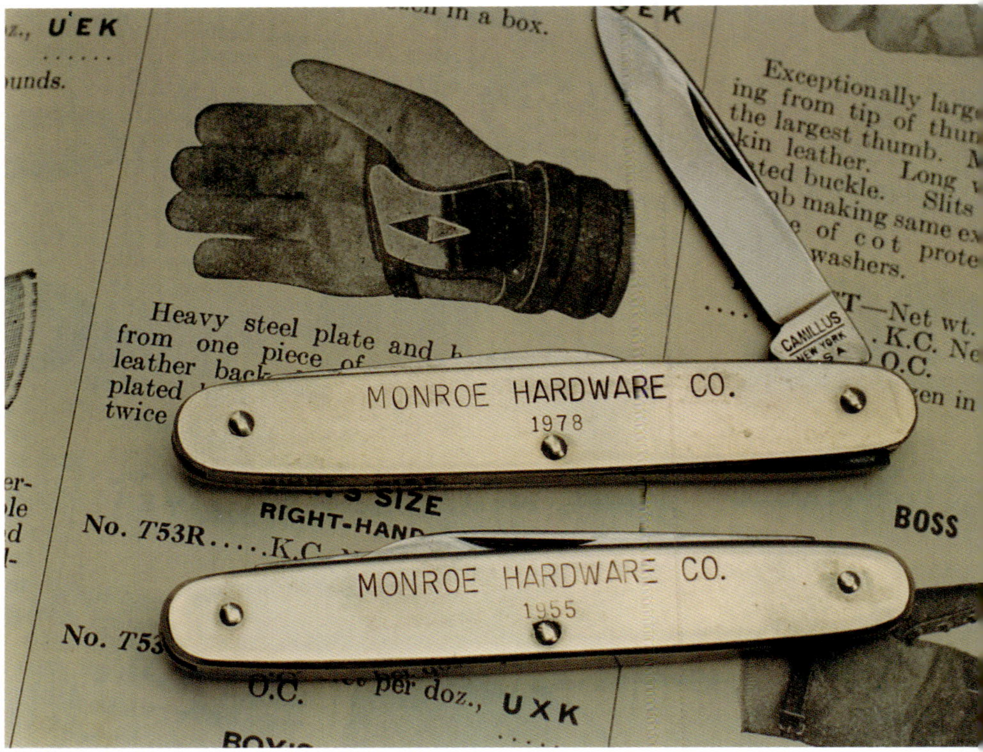

Above left: This letter opener features solid celluloid handles and unique advertising from the "First State Bank of Leola, South Dakota." In addition, it has a folding blade, often missed by buyers. Letter openers are not well established as a collectible so are relatively cheap to purchase. Value is $20–25.

Above right: These unique giveaways were made by the Camillus Cutlery Company for "Monroe Hardware" located in Monroe, North Carolina. One of these turned up in a flea market in Charlotte, North Carolina. The dates engraved are 1955 and 1978. This is an example of an outstanding recent piece of advertising. These metal-handled jack knives are an excellent addition to a collection and are valued at $40 each. According to an antique and gun collector who wrote to me from his hometown of Fayetteville, North Carolina, Monroe Hardware went out of business in the early 1980s, and that Monroe Hardware salesmen gave these knives out to retailers as a Christmas gift. The knives are made by Camillus Cutlery Company, a well-known and collected cutlery company.

Left: Robeson Cutlery Company was the producer of this metal-sided equal end pen advertising knife. "The Hallack & Howard Lumber Company" gave these knives away to customers and builders. As a company, Robeson Cutlery Company is widely collected across the United States. This adds greatly to the overall value of this knife. Because of its important tang stamping, near-mint condition and unique lumber yard advertisement, this knife has a value of $45–55.

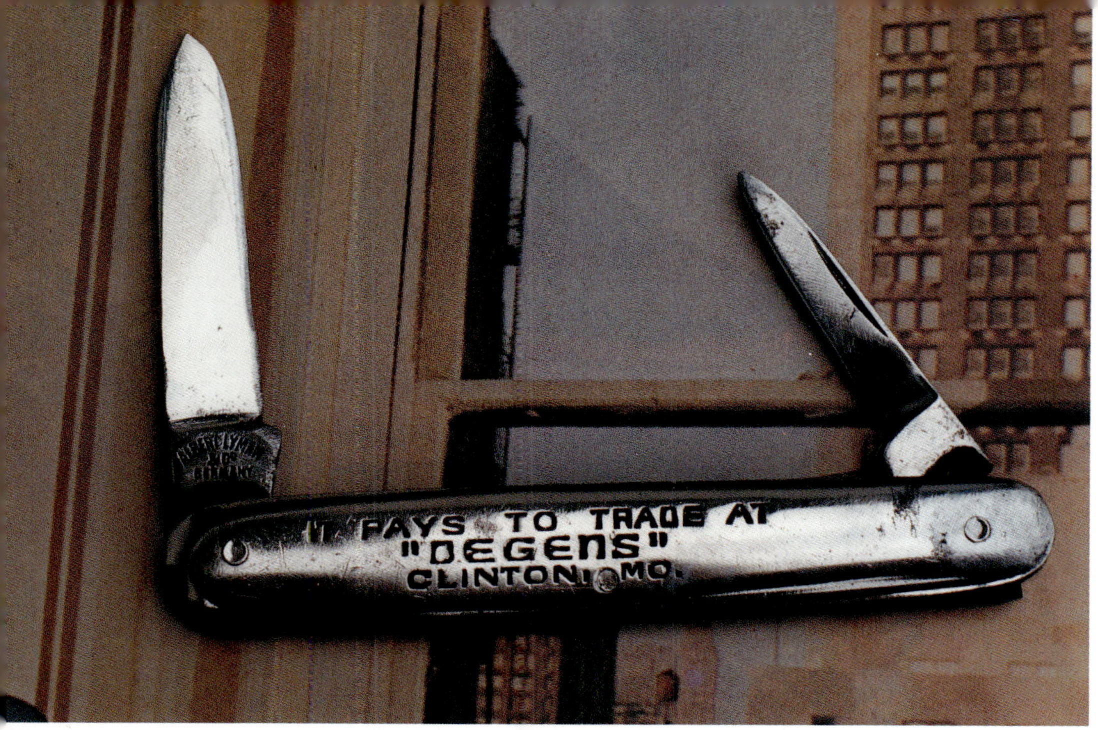

Left: Metal-handled knives with etched advertising are quite collectible. This example was made by "Albert Lyman & Co., Germany," probably in the 1920s. "Degens" was most likely a grocery store or general store located in Clinton, Mo. The unique slogan, "It pays to trade at Degens" adds to the value of the knife. Because the blades have seen moderate wear, this knife is valued at $30–35.

Below left: This unique advertiser was produced by Camillus Cutlery for *Woman's Home Companion* magazine. Because this particular Camillus stamping appears on four separate lines, we can establish the production date of this knife around World War II or before. This knife is handled in yellow cracked-ice celluloid, with brass emblem describing *Woman's Home Companion* as "The American Magazine."

Below right: The brass shield reads, in part, "Crowell Apprentice." This knife may have been produced for employees of this particular magazine as a reward for service to the company. Although the blades are tarnished, and show some wear, this knife is valued at $40–50, because of its rare advertising and age.

Made in Solingen, Germany, this advertiser was produced for the "Fuller Brush Company," most probably given to salesman for reaching particular sales goals. Certainly the "700" symbol appearing at both sides of the name Fuller is a significant sales goal. Value of this three-bladed knife with scissors is $25–30.

A knife almost identical to the Fuller knife above, this knife features cracked-ice celluloid, scissors, and a file blade. Given to customers by the "McWood Corporation," its value is $25–30.

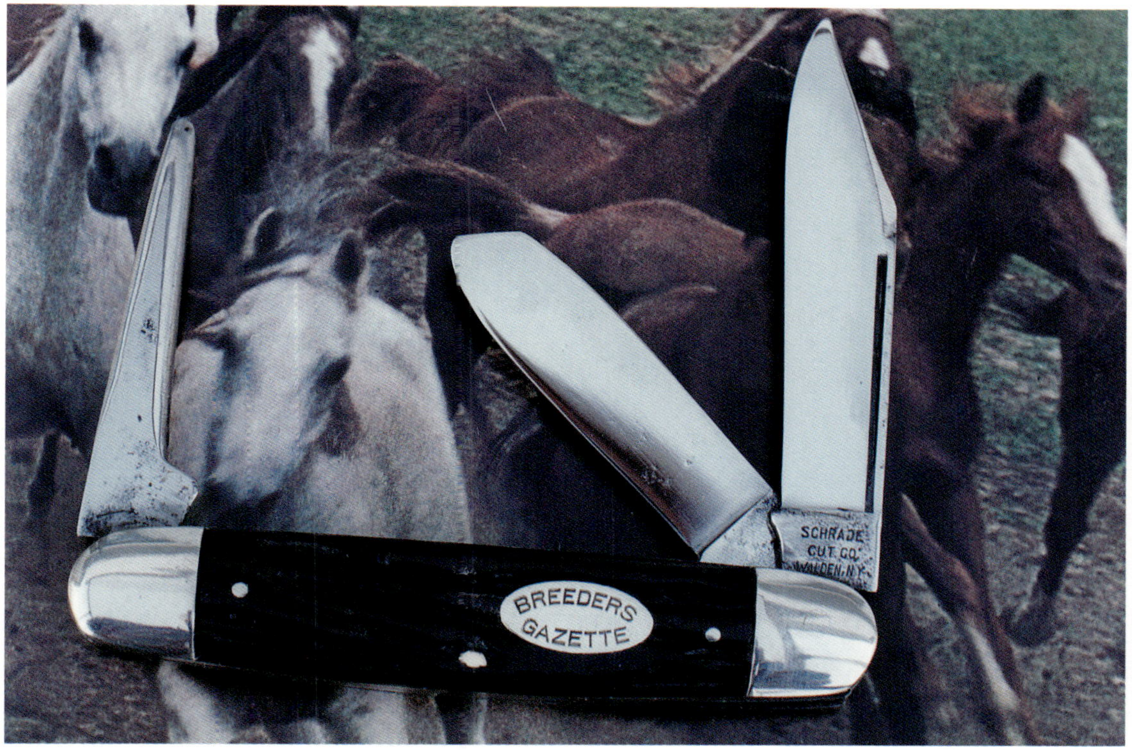

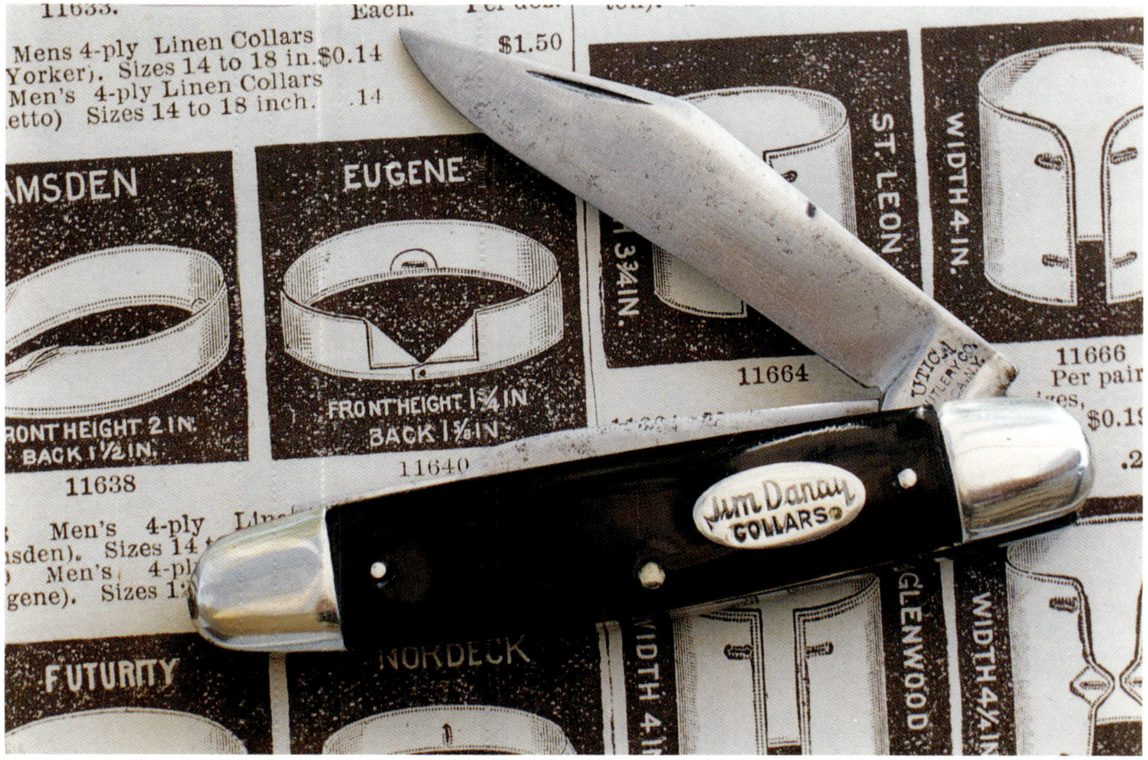

Above left: This three-bladed cattle pattern knife was made by the Schrade Cutlery Company most probably in the late 1930s and early 1940s. Although the term "cattle pattern" describes the general styles of this knife, it contains a leather punch, spey blade and master blade with long pull, all important blade styles for farmers and ranchers.

Above right: Handled in slick black celluloid, this knife's shield contrasts nicely against the dark celluloid. It reads "Breeders Gazette," a magazine put out by individuals involved in the cattle breeding industry. This periodical probably contained news about stud services, articles dealing with the results of recent auctions, medical updates, feeding practices, and general news about the raising and breeding of cattle. This knife is called an advertising "incentive knife." This means that this knife was given out as an incentive to those who subscribed to the *Breeders Gazette*. Incentive knives are a particular collecting category that is rapidly gaining popularity. With its unique shield, strong lettering, collectible pattern, and slick black celluloid, this knife has a value of $55–65.

Left: This knife actually advertises Jim Dandy *horse* collars. The slick black celluloid provides a striking background to the ad, which is placed in the shield. The Utica Cutlery Co. stamped in a curve on the tang of the master blade and the specific advertising places this knife in the time period 1910 to 1920. This two-bladed equal end jack is worth $55–65 in near-mint condition.

Above left: Since push blade knives are almost always mass produced for advertising purposes only, a significant collection of push blade advertising knives could be put together very inexpensively. This example is from "William Volker and Company, Home Furnishings since 1882." Significant blade wear detracts from the overall value of $10.

Above right: Another example of a keychain advertiser for the "Normandie Club, Gardena, California." For collectors of older night club and restaurant paraphernelia, this knife would have special significance. Probably made during the 1950s, its value is $12–18.

Left: An example of a mint advertiser for Peterson Appliance in Red Oak, Iowa, this serpentine jack is handled in cracked-ice celluloid. Although this knife advertises a local company, the famous General Electric "GE" symbol is prominently displayed near the tip bolster. With a phone number like "670" this knife probably dates back to the 1940s. It is an interesting collectible in outstanding shape. Value would be $20–25.

This keychain advertiser is unique because of the product it advertises. The Hudson automobile is shown in slogan and symbol form. Although the knife itself is quite inexpensively made, its old auto advertising makes it a valuable collectible. It is valued at $20, perhaps more to an auto aficionado.

Designed almost exactly like the Hudson auto advertiser, this knife is for a dealership which sells Hudson automobiles. The phone number, "Grand 0570," gives the viewer some indication of the age, probably 1940s or early 1950s. Made by the Utica Cutlery Company, the value is $20 because of its good condition, unique advertising, and well-known cutlery manufacturer.

V. BUSINESS & INDUSTRY

Above: This unique ruler knife was made for the "Midwest Machinery Manufacturing Corporation," located in Kansas City, Kansas. It would be a valuable giveaway to all machinists who use metric rulers constantly in setting up grinding and milling machines. Stamped "Executive" on the master blade, it is a product of the Colonial Cutlery Company, maker of knives since 1926.

Right: On the rear side of the Midwest Machinery advertising ruler knife, the metal sides are divided into inches and inch segments. 1/16-inch increments can be found on the top, and 1/32-inch increments are on the bottom. The value of this unique knife is $40–45, although it shows some blade wear which would lower the price somewhat.

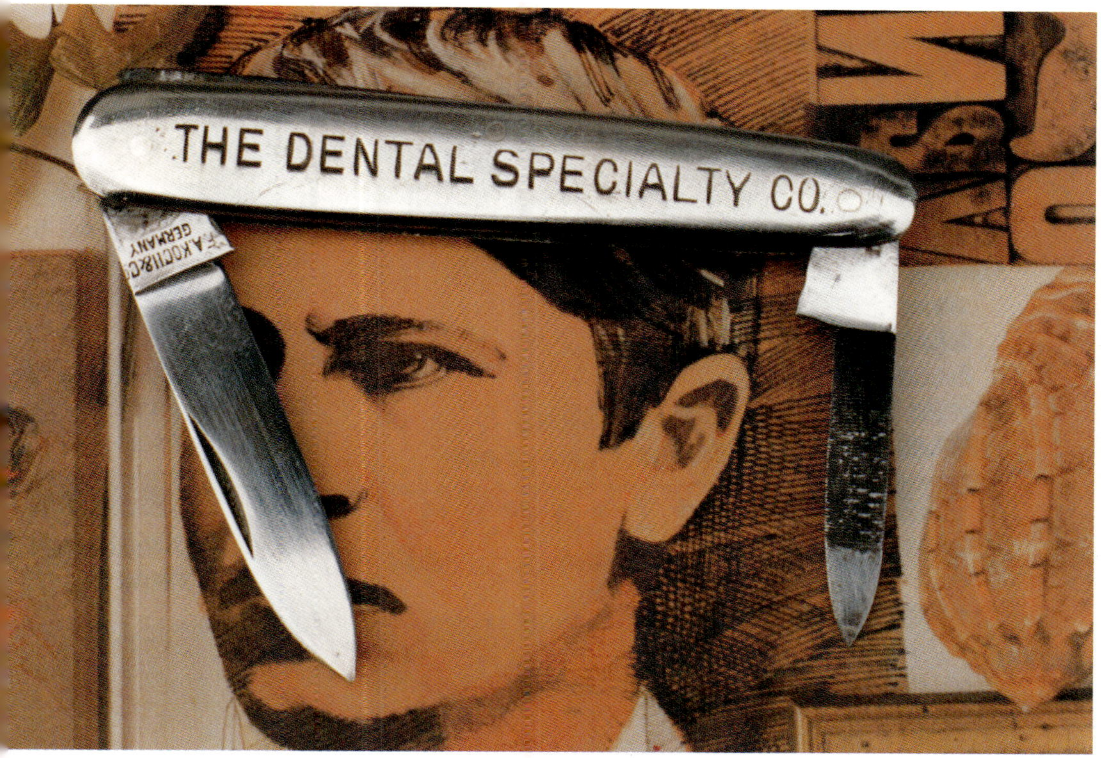

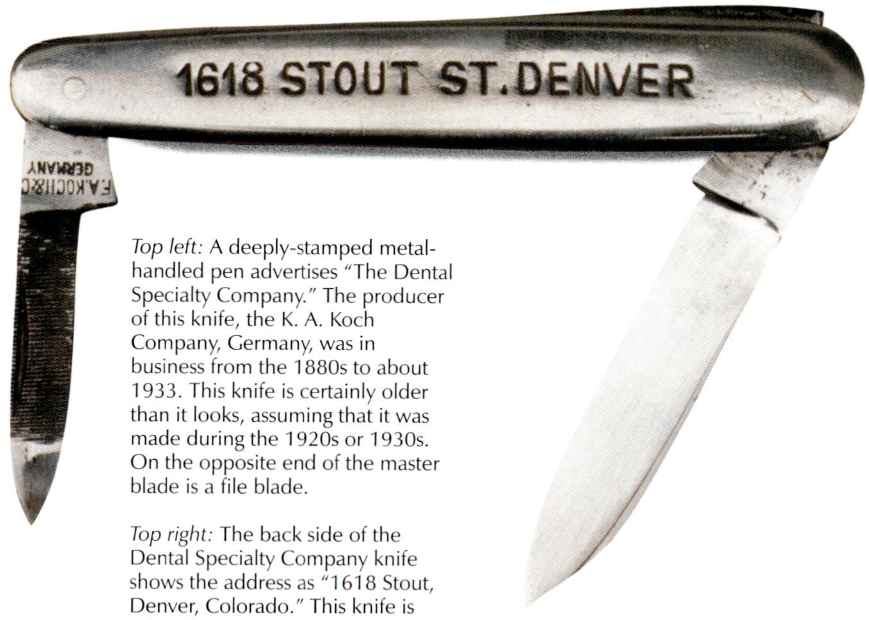

Top left: A deeply-stamped metal-handled pen advertises "The Dental Specialty Company." The producer of this knife, the K. A. Koch Company, Germany, was in business from the 1880s to about 1933. This knife is certainly older than it looks, assuming that it was made during the 1920s or 1930s. On the opposite end of the master blade is a file blade.

Top right: The back side of the Dental Specialty Company knife shows the address as "1618 Stout, Denver, Colorado." This knife is valued at $40–50 in its outstanding condition and unique advertising.

Bottom left: Metal-handled senator or equal end pens are certainly a very collectible group of advertising knives. Because of the bail attached, this one was designed to be put on a watch fob chain. The name "Cardwell" is not nearly as well-known as the second name, "Westinghouse," which was (and still is) a household name. Although this knife is basically unused, the pitting on the master blade lowers the price to $40–45.

Bottom right: The back handle of the Westinghouse senator pen shows the purpose of the advertising, "Friction Draft Gear." Made by Shapleigh Hardware, St. Louis, about 1940, this knife is valued both for the advertisement and the Shapleigh tang stamping.

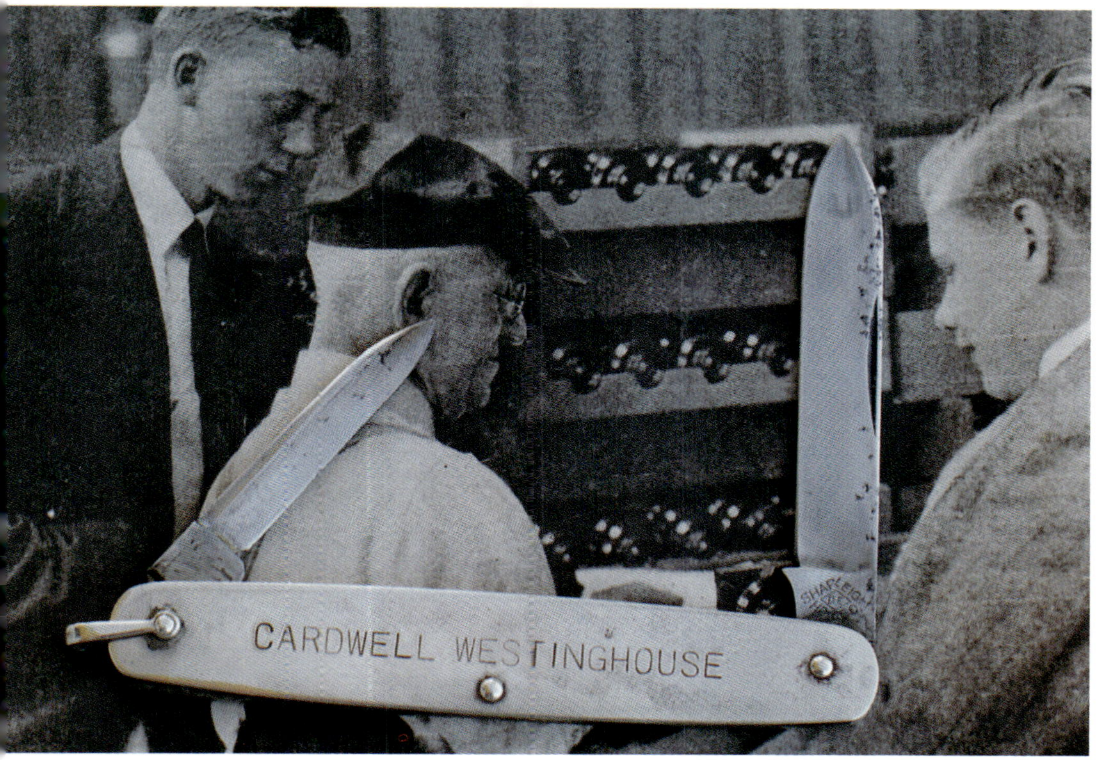

Above left: Unique because the name of the city and advertising company appear on the same side, this knife boldly advertises "The New England Newspaper Supply Co.," located in Worchester, Massachusetts. Schrade Walden Cutlery was the producer of this unique and very collectible knife. Value of this mint condition metal-handled advertiser with interesting city is $50–60.

Above right: Kutmaster is the contracted knife company for this well-made lobster pattern knife advertising the "Dakota Granite Company." The bail indicates that it is probably a watch fob chain attachment. It contains a fingernail file and nail cleaner along with the master blade. The advertising is unique, and South Dakota advertising is rare. Because Kutmaster is not an extremely collectible knife brand, the value is $25.

Left: Money clip knives were often given to salesmen who reached or exceeded certain sales goals. This knife was given by the "P & A" or Parts and Accessories sales managers. Made by Imperial or Colonial (among others), its collector value is generally limited to those in the auto industry. Value $12–15.

Above left: This advertiser is called a "tip bolster" one-bladed jack knife, given to special customers by the Scarville (Iowa) Grain Elevator. Made by in the 1940s, it is in mint condition. Scarville is certainly a unique town name. The advertisement for coal helps date this particular advertiser, which is valued at $25–30.

Above right: This advertiser for "Hillyard Chemical Company" of St. Louis was made by Camillus Cutlery Company, one of many cutlery companies commissioned by Hillyard to produce advertising knives. The master blade shows the Camillus "Sword Brand" stamping, one of many Camillus stampings. Hillyard Chemical produced a wide variety of cleaning, polishing, and other chemical products. It is fairly common among advertising pieces. This example is handled in cracked-ice celluloid, and has a value of $35–40.

Right: The small pen blade of the Hillyard Chemical advertiser clearly shows the tang stamping "Camillus Cutlery Company, Camillus, New York." The stamping is contained on four lines. This is known to collectors as a "Camillus 4-line," a stamping used during or before the 1940s. The stamping contained on four separate lines is a good indication of a World War II-era production knife, important to collectors of military cutlery.

Above left: This equal end pen with tip bolsters, handled in blue celluloid, was also commissioned by Hillyard Chemical. The advertisement is contained in the unique nickel silver shield. "Shine All" was one of the products produced by Hillyard Chemical, located in St. Joseph, Missouri.

Above right: The reverse side of the Hillyard Chemical advertising knife shows a second shield raised above the handle material. The shield is made in the form of a can of "Shine All" chemical. This advertising knife was made by the Stainless Cutlery Company of New York, a company in business from 1924 to the 1930s. The value of this unique piece is $40–45.

Left: This mint, bolsterless advertising knife for Hillyard Chemicals was made by the very famous Western States Cutlery Company, originally located in Boulder, Colorado, probably in the late 1940s or 1950s. It is handled in yellow cracked-ice celluloid, and contains a watch fob bail. Because of its extremely desirable tang stamping, mint condition, and very clear advertising, it is valued at $70–75 or slightly more. The master blade shows the recognizable curved "Western States Cutlery" stamping.

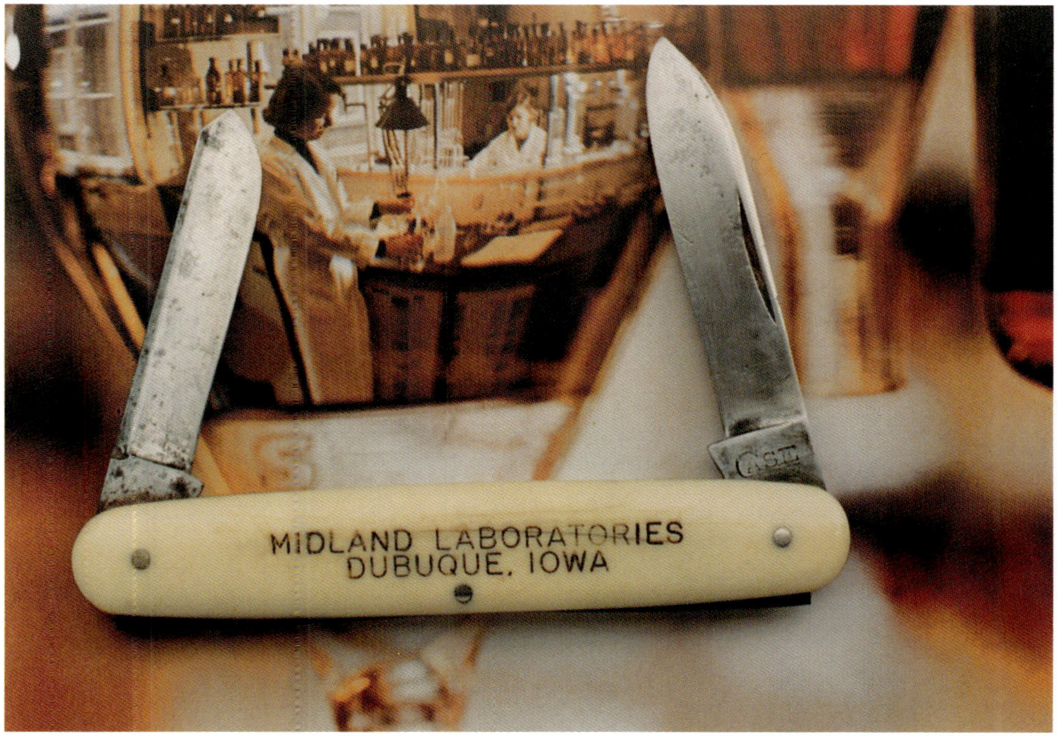

Above left: Hillyard Chemical Corporation had a sales division which marketed the various chemical products produced by the company. This advertiser, a small bartender's knife with corkscrew and cap lifter master blade bears the advertisement from the "Hillyard Sales Company" located in St. Joseph, Missouri. The knife is handled in cracked-ice celluloid, and was made by Camco, a stamping used by the Camillus Cutlery Company. Its value is $20–25.

Above right: One of the smallest advertisers, this swell end jack knife was designed to be hung on a key chain. It advertises the "Newton Manufacturing Company," as the red lettering indicates, and was made by Colonial Knife Company, a common manufacturer of advertising knives. Its value is $10.

Left: This two-bladed knife handled in french ivory celluloid advertises "Midland Laboratories" of Dubuque, Iowa. This style is often referred to as an "office knife," although not etched as most office knives are. This is an old knife, as evidenced by the Case Tested stamping on the master blade. It dates from as early as the 1920s to about 1940. Early Case knives with full blades and very readable advertising are valued at $70–75.

Right: This is a push blade knife, since the blade pushes out from the end of the handle. This example advertises "Rocky Mountain Paint." The phone number gives us a clue as to its fairly recent production. Value would be $10–12.

Below left: Handled in cracked-ice celluloid, this advertiser for the "Anderson Bit Service" is in mint condition. Made by the Western Cutlery and stamped "Western Boulder" on the master blade, it is a unique collectible. Because Western Cutlery knives are well-collected, and because this knife is in pristine mint condition, it has a value of $70–80.

Below right: Another "tip bolster" advertiser also handled in cracked-ice celluloid. Probably from the 1950s or early 1960s, this knife has very readable graphic lettering for the "A. H. Davies Printing Company." It is valued at $20.

This lobster pattern advertiser for the "Stovall Construction Company" effectively uses yellow cracked-ice and red celluloid to set off their advertisement. Located in Dallas, Texas, their main business is "Power Line Construction," as indicated on the front of the knife. The value of this knife in near-mint condition is $25–30.

Uniquely designed for use by pharmacists, this knife sports a very flexible spatula in addition to its regular blade. The spatula was used by pharmacists to sort and count pills when dispensing prescriptions. This advertiser was almost certainly given to pharmacists by drug manufacturer "reps." The advertisement for "Tums" is well-known.

The rear side of the Tums advertising spatula knife again admonishes pharmacists to display their product. This knife is quite large by pocketknife standards, almost eight inches with blade open. In all probability, however, it would not be carried in a pocket like other pocketknives. Made by the Ulster Cutlery Company, its value is $45–55 because of its unique design, well-known advertisement, and rarity.

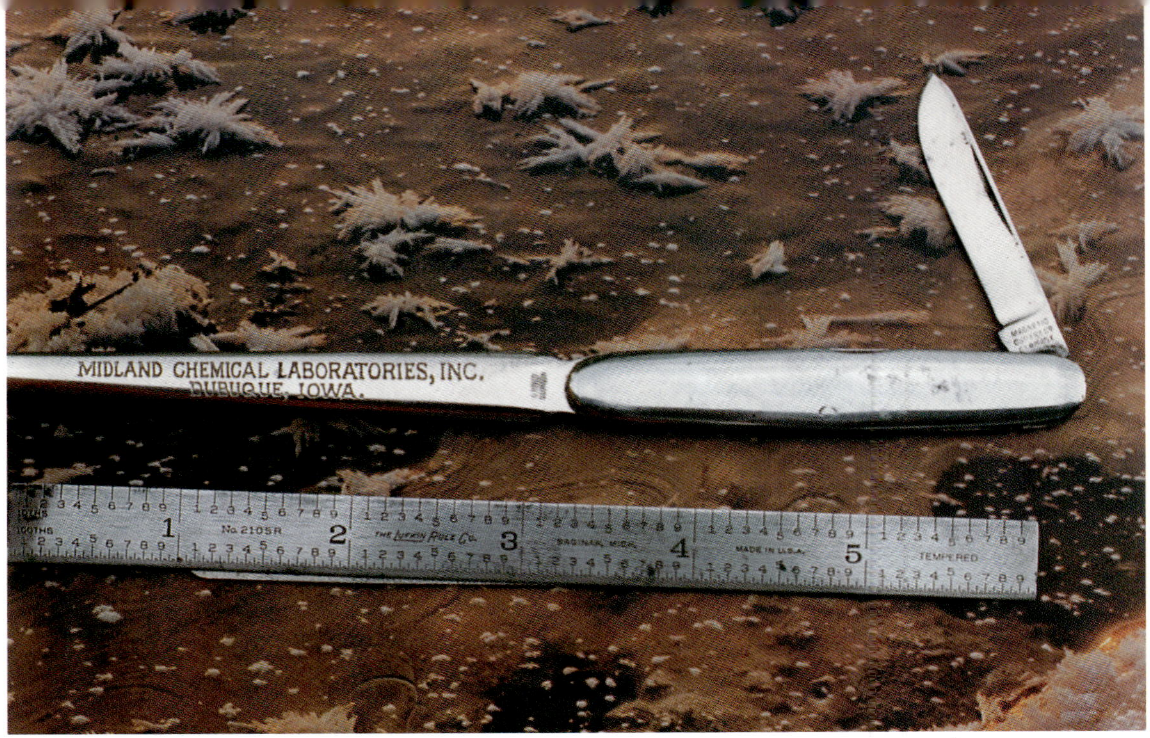

Top: This letter opener is issued by the Midland Chemical Laboratories, Inc. located in Dubuque, Iowa. Produced by the Magnetic Cutlery Company, circa 1900 to 1932, it is all-metal, and like most advertising pieces, was given out by salesmen during normal sales routes. Normally, the advertising appears on the handle, not on the blade. The value is $25–30.

Bottom: The famous "Keen Kutter" tang stamping on this "Dowell" Corporation advertiser is perhaps more important to knife collectors than to advertising collectors, although advertising knives with good pedigrees are certainly more valuable. Cracked-ice handles appear on this equal end pen. The product produced by Dowell Corp. is unknown. Value of the knife is affected by the rough blade condition and unknown product and is set at $20–25.

Above: This unique metal-sided equal end pen knife advertises the 100th anniversary of the Disston Saw and Tool Company. The company started in 1840; this knife was issued in 1940. Advertising memorabilia which celebrates the centennial or one hundred year anniversaries of any company are unique, and have a premium attached to the value. The tang of the master blade is stamped "Disston" also, revealing little about the manufacturer of the knife, although Camillus made numerous knives on contract.

Above right: The reverse of the Disston anniversary knife gives us further clues about this anniversary piece. It was issued by the "Reichman-Crosby Company, Memphis, Tennessee," which I assume to be a tool distributor or hardware store. The knife is in pristine mint condition, that is, unused and unsharpened, and is an especially important acquisition to tool collectors nationwide. A similar example, shown and purchased at a national tool show sold for $100. Although the tool collectors take special interest in these marked items, such sales provide real pricing data.

Right: These two small advertisers come from Denver, Colorado. Both were produced in the 1930s or earlier, as indicated by the phone number on the "Windsor Farm" knife. The "Michaelson's" knife is an example of a very early "butterfly" knife in which the blade folds out from the center. The bail holds the two sides of the handle together. The value of this knife is $30–35. The Winsor Farm knife is valued at $20–25.

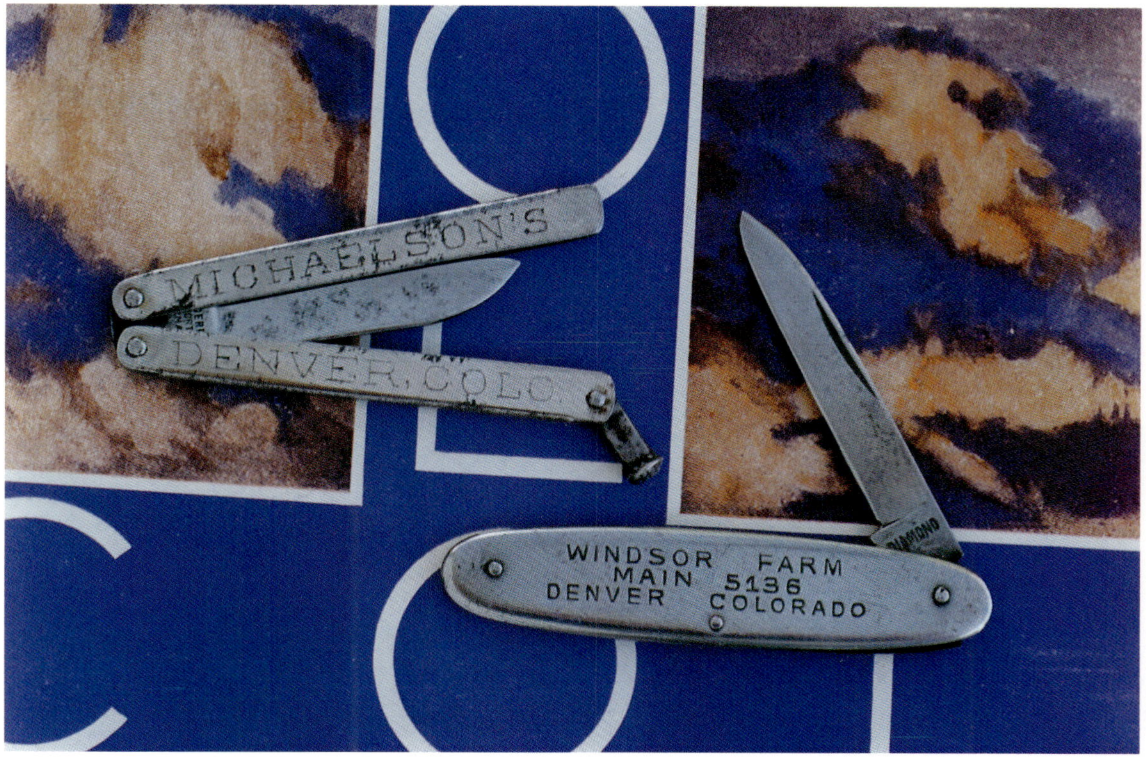

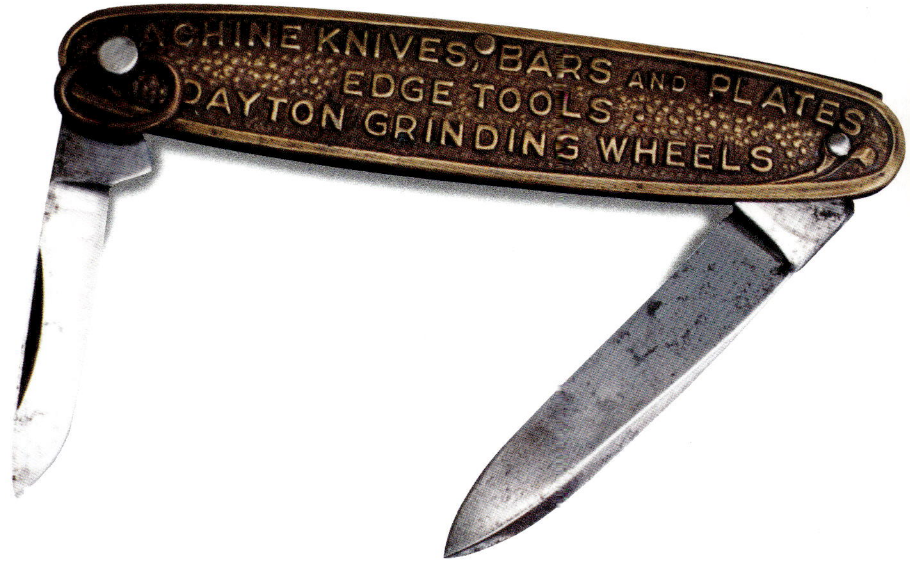

Above left: The Simonds, Worden, White Company in Dayton, Ohio gave away very unique pen knives. They are ring turn openers, meaning that the blades can be opened simply by turning the metal rings attached to each blade. For employees of a typical machine shop, with broken fingernails and greasy hands, the opening mechanism on these knives was a blessing. Ring turn opening knives are very rare and quite collectible.

Above right: In addition to the ring turn, this knife is valuable because it is brass-sided with raised lettering, the most desirable form of metal sided advertisers. It advertises machine knives, grinding tools, and edge tools, materials frequently found in the milling industry. The tang stamp on the master blade reads simply "SWW," an abbreviation of the company name. Who produced these knives is a mystery, although some research indicates that Camillus Cutlery Company was the producer. The value, based on the condition, unique raised lettering and opening style is $75, and sure to appreciate higher.

Left: Infrequently, letter openers were made with a knife built into the handle. These knives are often overlooked by collectors. This opener advertises the "American Gear Company" with its block lettering stamped into the green handle material. Without a cutlery name to determine its original manufacture, this opener is valued at $15–20 because of its excellent condition and strong lettering.

Above left: This is an example of a shell-handled knife, the plastic advertising sheet wrapped around the metal knife shell. The advertisement is for the "Premier" company, with offices in Cleveland, Los Angeles, Atlanta, and Toronto. These knives are cheaply made, and the appeal to advertising collectors is only because of the potential familiarity of the advertisement. Value is $10.

Above right: A most unique advertiser, made for the "Gilbert Printing Company, Boyertown, Pennsylvania." Shaped like a number "1," this knife is sure to attract attention, and is a unique advertising giveaway. Bearing a Colonial Cutlery stamping, it is inexpensively made. Value $15–20.

Right: Although the company advertised is located in Chicago, Illinois, the knife was made in Sweden. Richly engraved with snakes or dragons entwined around the end pins, this knife is very well-made. With only three names on engraved on the sides, the purpose of the advertiser is unknown. Unique styling and well-made knife in outstanding condition give this knife a value of $55–65.

Left: With the inscription of "MAGNA" on the blade, and "The Elegant" written in script on the metal sides of this equal end pen, this knife is full of intrigue. The knife was made in Solingen, Germany, by the Koeller and Company, a company which started as early as the mid 1800s. Magna was one of their regular stampings, and probably does not advertise a particular product. Made in the 1940s or 1950s, we do not know what "The Elegant" advertises—perhaps a nightclub or restaurant. Value is $30–40, perhaps more if additional research could track down the specific advertisement.

Below left: Rarely do collectors see knives which have the quality of this pearl-handled Remington. Strong blade etching almost always indicates "pristine mint" condition; a very rare commodity for a knife over 50 years old. Because pearl is quite fragile, and easily broken if dropped, unbroken pearl handles are rare for any knife. This two-bladed "equal end" pen is truly a unique advertising example.

Below right: A closeup of the pearl-handled Remington shows the deeply etched advertisement, "Furness-Bermuda Line," inked in blue. Most probably, this was a steamship company which traveled between islands located near Bermuda. The blue flying flag with the "B" is also an indication that this was a steamship company, as flags are frequently associated with ships. The value of this advertising knife is based on four factors: its Remington stamping, the mint condition, the unbroken pearl handles, and its most striking advertisement. This combination gives this knife a value of $150–175.

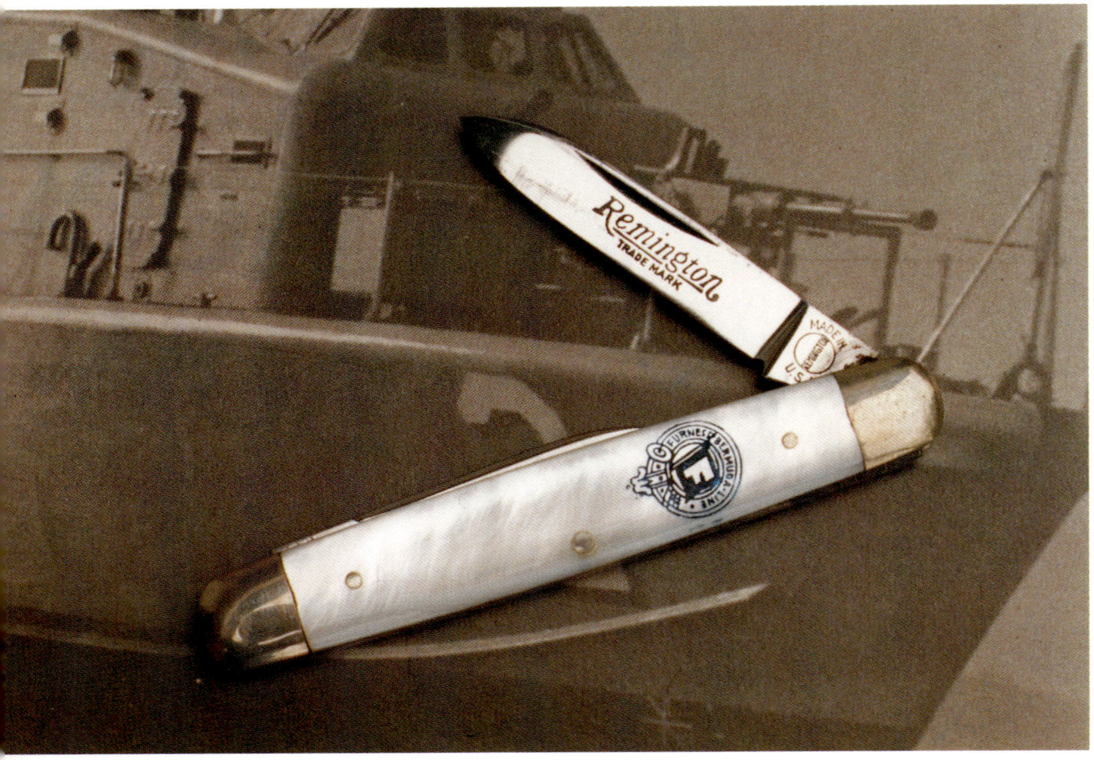

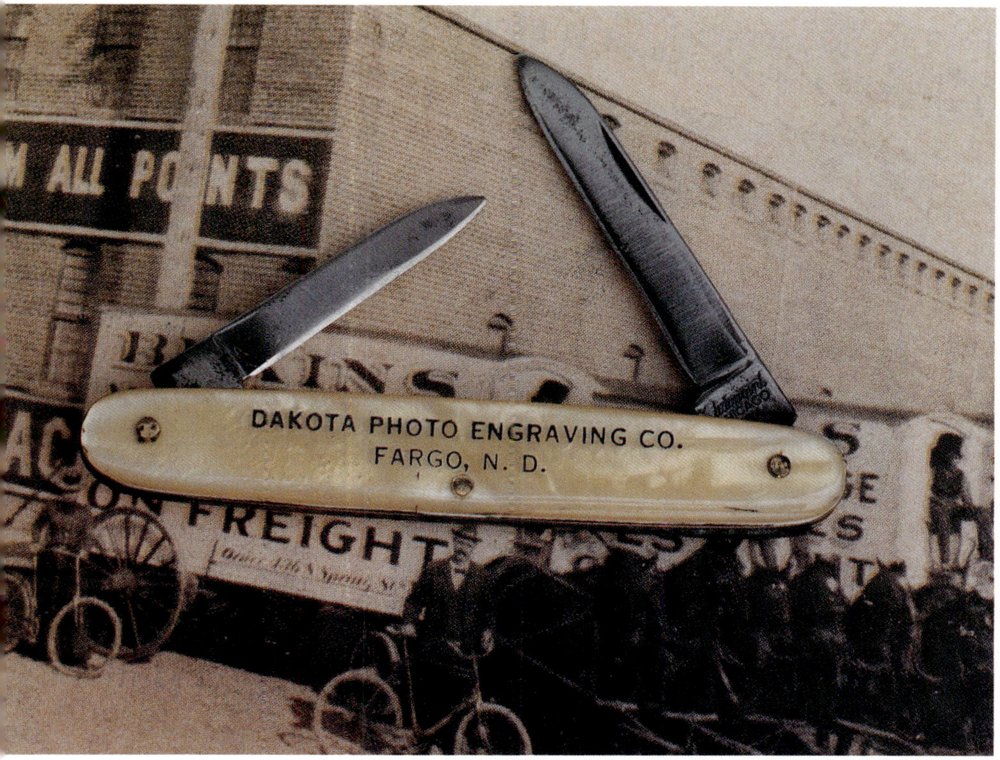

Above left: Handled in cracked-ice celluloid, this lobster pattern boasts two blades and a long fingernail file. The advertisement for "Lucey" is inset into the celluloid sides as a knife "shield." The red insert with gold lettering makes a striking contrast to the lighter celluloid. Value is $25–30.

Above right: "The Osborne Company" is the stamping on this equal end, metal-sided advertising knife made by Camillus Cutlery. The master blade is stamped "Camco," Camillus's secondary brand stamping. Value of this knife in its excellent condition is $35–40, perhaps more if the advertisement could be identified.

Left: Cracked-ice celluloid is the handle material used on this equal end pen knife made by the Autopoint Company, Chicago, Illinois. Autopoint was in business from 1911 to 1979. Fargo, North Dakota was the location of the "Dakota Photo Engraving Company." Because of the wear on both blades, this knife is worth between $15–20. The yellow celluloid provides an excellent background for showing off the lettering.

Above: Although the blades are worn from use and sharpening, this two-bladed equal end pen knife contains a unique nickel silver shield advertising "Shuler and Benninghofen, Hamilton, Ohio." This is obviously a local company, whose product or service is unknown. Its value lies in its jigged bone handles, and sharply engraved advertising shield. It is valued at $35–40.

Above right: Lobster pen knives, often with a money clip attached to the other side, were made to advertise various automotive products. Modern printing techniques can produce outstanding graphics. This example, engraved "Altronics," was given to automobile dealers and mechanics who purchased these ignition parts. Value is $12–18.

Right: These authentic Victorinox knives, stamped "Burlington Northern" and "CNGT" are both railroad advertisements, and appeal to not only cutlery but railroad collectors. Very well-made, these useful advertisers are worth $10–20 each.

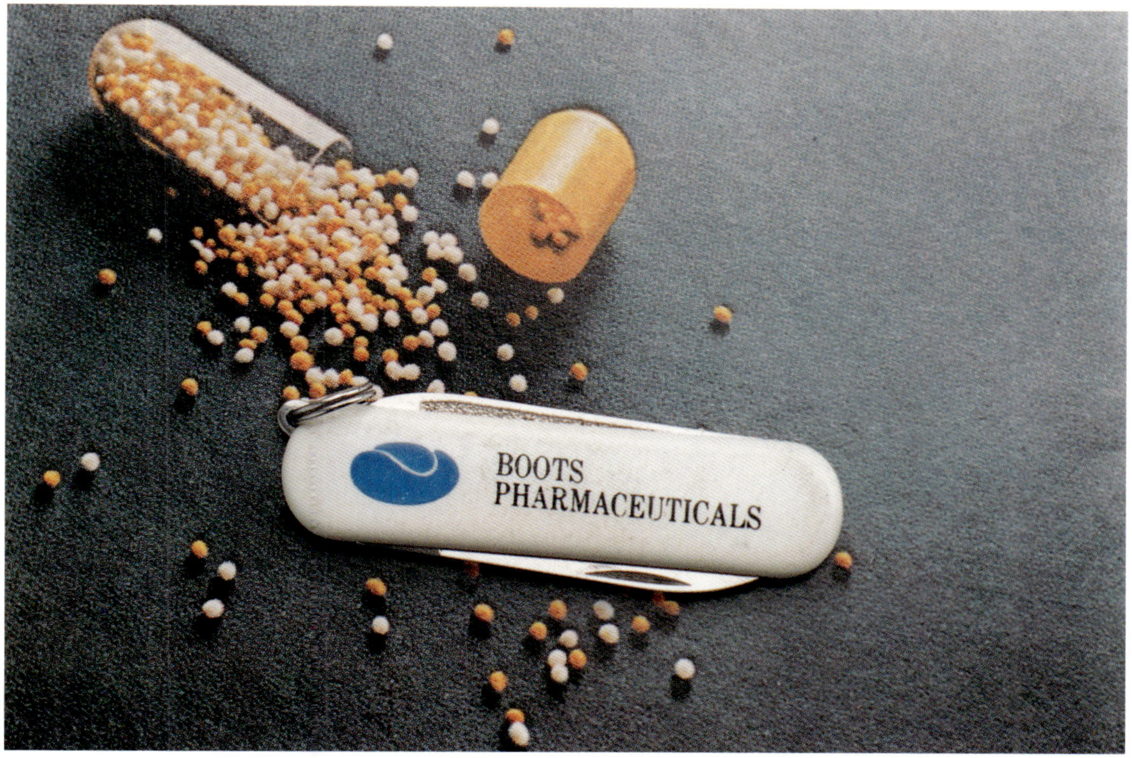

An interesting collection of Victorinox knives with different advertising could be put together with examples from different industries. This one is for "Boots Pharmaceuticals," and has a value of $10–20.

"Syntex" is a pharmaceutical production corporation located in Colorado. According to the advertising, the company gave this knife away to employees in the plant for completing 2 million safe (accident free) working hours. This advertising incentive appeals to collectors of Victorinox advertising knives or those individuals collecting industrial advertising. Value is $10–20.

Above left: Western Cutlery, Boulder, Colorado was the producer for this cracked-ice celluloid-handled cutlery advertiser, given as a safety award in 1952. As indicated earlier, all Western Cutlery knives are becoming more valuable in their own right, especially the earlier Western Boulder and Western States stampings. With strong advertising on the knife the overall value is increased. Its unique advertisement, date, mint condition, and good cutlery pedigree raise its value to $65–75.

Above right: A closeup of the shield on the Western safety award knife shows the company who issued the award. In this case, "Climax Molybdenum Company" located in the mountains of Colorado. Climax Molybdenum is an important Colorado company, and it makes sense that they would choose Western as the producer of this unique knife.

Right: Kanorado is located just inside the Kansas state line on Interstate 70. This advertiser for "Coffey-Reid, Inc.," was given to those involved in the natural resources industry. The advertising is printed on a plastic sheet and glued to the metal knife shell. Cheaply made, its value is $10.

Right: The Barlow knife is one of the oldest knife styles. Strongly built, these styles were designed for hard use. This example, made by Colonial, is of recent vintage, probably the 1970s, and advertises "Lake Charles. Shlumberger." Because this advertisement is only printed, not etched, on the white plastic handle, it will be worn off if the knife is used for any length of time. This advertisement is of local interest, and has a value of $15–20.

Below left: Cracked-ice celluloid seems to be the handle material of choice for many companies. This "peanut" style of knife advertises "The Freese Metal Products Corporation, Lancaster, Pennsylvania." Lancaster is in the heart of Amish country, and this company may have served the Amish. Made by Camillus, this knife is well-made, and has a value of $25–30 in mint condition.

Below right: Not only does this advertising knife for "Morrell Manufacturing, St. Louis, Missouri" have both the name of the company and the location on the same side, but it possesses a unique figural shape. Baseball bat-shaped knives, like all figural advertisers, are quite valuable, and rare in good condition with unbroken celluloid handles. This advertising knife is valued as between $35–45.

Top: This lobster watch fob knife was an advertiser for the "Union Pacific Railroad." Designed to fit on a railroad watch, it was produced by the famous Remington Cutlery Company which went out of business in 1941. Made of cracked-ice celluloid, this example is not in the best of condition with cracks in the celluloid and faded advertising emblem. In excellent shape, it would be worth $65 because of its famous emblem and famous Remington pedigree; in this condition, however, it is worth about $25.

Bottom: Pearl knives in good condition without broken pearl are becoming a very rare commodity. Add to the pearl handles a unique design, and you have a valuable cutlery piece. This knife is called a "spatula" knife, used only by two occupations. Most were used by physicians and pharmacists to mix various ointments and medicines, using knives which contained both a spatula blade and regular blade. The second use was by painters to mix oil paints on a pallette. This example contains the faint advertising etching "George Epham Colors, East St. Louis." Value, based on rare design, pearl handle, and unique etching, is $100–125.
This example was made by Cattaraugus Cutlery Company.

Above left: Thousands of companies used cutlery as a means of advertising products. Cutlery products were well-received by the public, and the advertisement was read each and every time the user took the knife out of their pocket. The "Selig Company" is but one of these thousands of companies. This equal end pen has tip bolsters, and was made by Camco, the cheaper brand stamping of the Camillus Cutlery Company, in the early 1950s to 1960s. Looking at the cities stamped into the celluloid, the Selig Company served the major cities in the Southern portion of the United States.

Above right: The reverse of the Selig Company advertising giveaway gives the collector a clue to the product produced by Selig. "Modern Sanitation since 1896" is the slogan. Cleaners used to sanitize homes and business were most likely the products produced by Selig. Value is $20–25.

Left: Schrade Walden Cutlery Company was the producer of this electrician's two-bladed jack with "I. T. E. Circuit Breaker Co." stamping. Black celluloid, the handle material of this knife, was discontinued in approximately the early 1960s or before, even though Schrade was still using the "Schrade Walden" stamping into the early 1970s. This knife, with a locking screwdriver-wire stripper combination blade is designed around a very famous military knife called the TL-29. "TL" stands for "tool lineman," a military designation for the type of two-bladed knife used in the military by field linemen, electricians, and related fields. This knife has a value of $35–45 because of its use of black celluloid, its mint condition, and Schrade Walden stamping.

Left: This unique bladed tool is technically not a knife, but a tool used to open the backs of pocket watches by watch repairmen. As such, it serves an important and very specific function. The advertising is very striking, put out by the Hamilton Watch Company. The raised shield, famous motto, and lettering make this a real collector's item. Although somewhat difficult to price because of its rarity and uniqueness, the value would be around $30–40.

Below left: Advertising knives with special shapes make an interesting collection. In this case, three knives—two shaped like keys, and a third like a huge bolt—make an attractive display. These knives range in value from $15–35, depending upon the maker of the knife and the importance of the advertisement.

Below right: A closeup of the special "bolt-shaped" knife. The avertised products—bolts, nails, hangers, tools—are printed on the bolt knife. These knives were given by salesmen to customers, commercial contracts, or retail companies. Value $20–30.

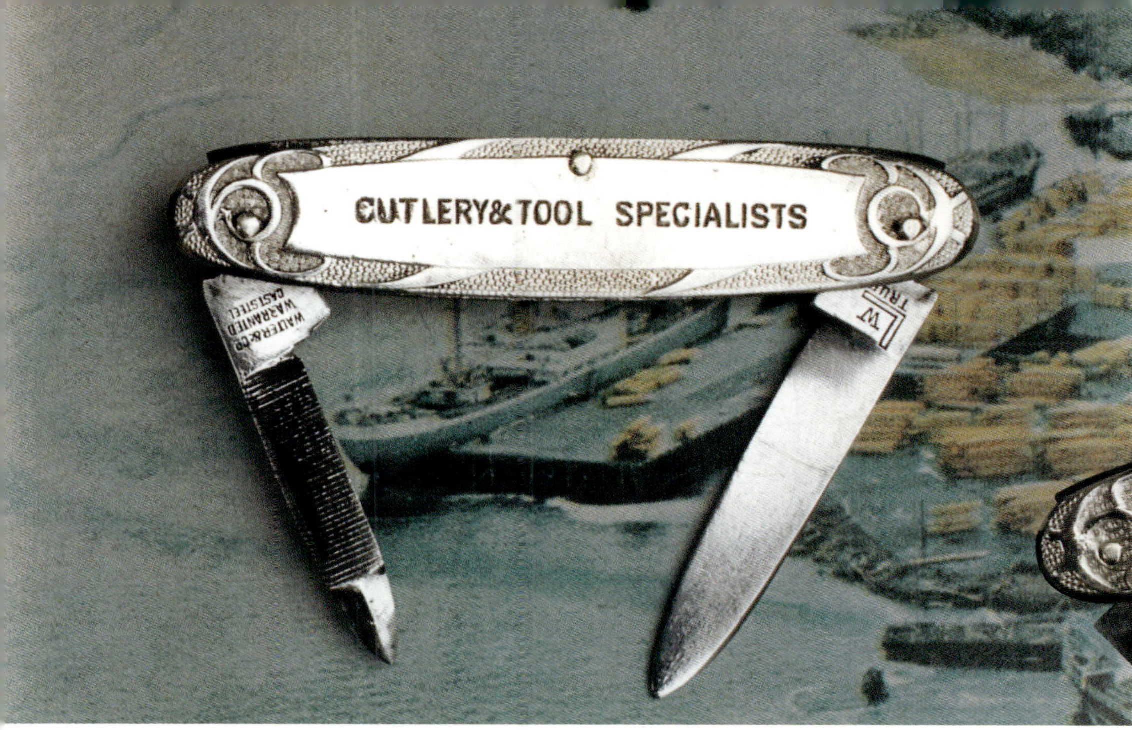

Above left: Inscribed and engraved bolsters adorn this unique, metal-sided pen knife made for "Forbes and Van Horn, LTD." This two-blade equal end pen contains a fingernail file as a second blade. In addition to its fancy decoration, the company name and location in Vancouver, British Columbia make this a rare find.

Above right: The specialty of the Forbes and Van Horn company is etched on the back handle of this knife. "Cutlery and Tool Specialists" reads the engraved advertisement. The tang stamping is etched "Walter and Company," a British firm which made knives in the 1920s. Value is $40–50.

Left: This strange wood-handled knife is strongly stamped "Ontario Pacific," presumably a Canadian Railroad. This knife was probably used by railroad workers, and was not an advertising giveaway piece. Its use is unknown, although its length of around 6 inches would be valuable in stripping wire or opening boxes of supplies. Because of its rarity and unique stamping, its value is $15, perhaps more to a collector of railroad memorabilia.

Above left: Sample knives were made by cutlery companies to show potential clients the size, shape, and specific printing appearances available, in this case, the "Robertson's Merc. Inc." This red printing on yellow cracked-ice celluloid is quite striking. Notice that this sample is numbered "L-52," and has been described by the cutlery company as a "sales builder." Whether these samples are more or less valuable than actual advertising knives is an interesting question. Value is $20–30.

Above right: An interesting advertiser with an interesting shape. Like other knives which have specialty shapes, this knife looks like a fan belt and cardboard package. A unique advertiser for "Gates Rubber Company," located in Denver, Colorado, this knife is in mint condition. Of recent Japanese vintage, the value is $25–35.

Right: R. Groves and Sons, Sheffield, was the producer of this simple but elegant metal advertising knife, etched simply "Teacher." Whether it was one of a number of knives displaying occupations is not known. Its quality is outstanding, and as a teacher, it has a special meaning to me. It has been suggested that the name "Teacher" might refer to a liquor brand by the same name. Its mint condition, Sheffield make, and unique stamping places the value of $50–60.

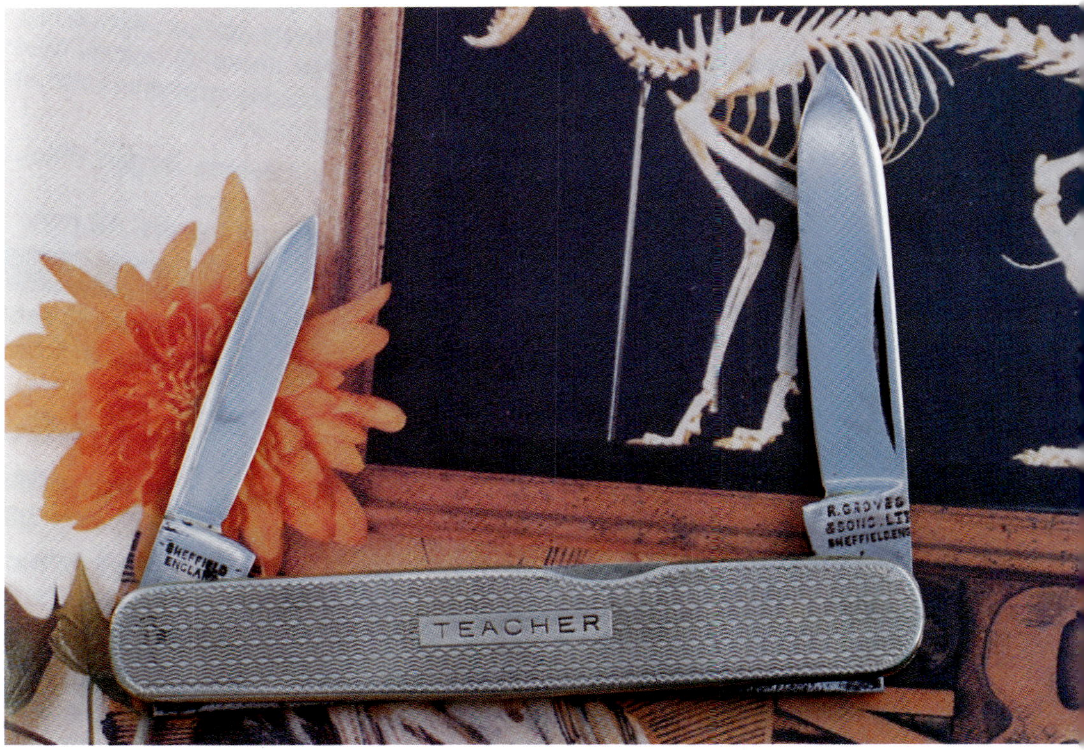

Above left: Metal advertising jacks in mint condition are always premium knives. This one was made by the George Worstenholm Cutlery Company of Sheffield England. Worstenholm used the "I*XL" logo which stood for "I Excel." This knife has the famous logo etched into the master blade; a sign of pristine mint knives. The advertising is also extremely unique, reading "Atlas Asbestos Co., Ltd., Montreal and Toronto." Canadian advertising knives are rarely found, and asbestos companies are almost non-existent today. Canada imported most of their cutlery from Great Britian, as seen in this example.

Above right: The rear of the "Atlas Asbestos Company" advertiser describes the various products produced by this Canadian company. "Asbestos goods, packings, pipe coverings, etc." are all produced by Atlas. This example was probably produced in the 1930s or 1940s, and has been stored since that time. In addition to its I*XL logo, the Worstenholm slogan, "oil the joints," is imprinted on the back of the blade, an important factor in preventing excessive blade wear. This example, in mint condition with unique advertising on both sides and famous cutlery manufacturer, is worth $65–75.

Left: Another Canadian advertiser uses celluloid handles to completely enclose the backspring on this two-bladed pen knife. Using the famous Canadian maple leaf inlaid in the celluloid, the advertisement reads "Brunner Mono Canada Limited." The particular product advertised on this knife is unknown. The advertiser, in mint condition, is unique and valued at $40–50.

Above: Baseball bat advertisers are always collectible, although this one is rather cheaply made with the handle material a thin plastic stretched over a metal shell. It advertises "Seneca Seat Cover Center, Wichita, Kansas." Its unsharpened condition helps increase its value to the $15–20 range.

Above right: The slogan of the Seneca Seat Cover Center carries the baseball theme also. "It's a hit when you let Joe do it." Although the word "it" has been worn off, the message is clear. The plastic covering on this advertiser looks like real wood—a unique feature.

Right: This cutlery salesman's plastic case is loaded with samples showing how various cutlery advertising could be used on different knife styles. The products and companies included are not yet real advertising pieces, but potential examples. Included are some very famous companies such as Jeep, Admiral, U-Haul, Maytag, and IGA. Value of this salesman's cutlery sample case (the top left example is not an original) is $65–75.

"Trane" is a company famous for selling and installing air conditioning units. This example is a bone-handled trapper pattern—certainly rare for advertising knives. In addition to the company name and symbol, the words "XL 1200" appear on the front. Made by the American Blade Cutlery Company, it has a value of $35–45.

The rear side of the Trane Air Conditioning Company advertiser shows the purpose of this knife. The rear side is stamped "Christmas 1986." This advertiser was obviously a Christmas gift to valued customers in 1986.

Handled in yellow cracked-ice celluloid, this mint two-bladed jack was made by the Camillus Cutlery Company. The advertisement engraved on the shield reads "The Everstick Anchor Company." With the stamping of the cutlery company name on four lines, this knife was most probably made in the 1940s. Its value is $35–45.

The rear of the Everstick Anchor Company knife is unique because it has a second shield embedded into the celluloid. This shield is the company logo, reading "The Anchor of Merit." Usually, knife shields are included only on the front side of the knife.

VI. PETROLEUM RELATED PRODUCTS

"Resource Drilling" is the company name, etched, probably by laser, into the wooden handle material of this large Gerber lockback. Gerber is a well-known name in the knife business, and this lockback is well-made and sturdy enough to handle the types of jobs which exist in the oil fields. This Gerber advertiser has a value of $45–55.

Left: "Havoline Motor Oil" is the advertiser illustrated on this mint lockback knife. Produced by the Western Cutlery Company in their Longmont, Colorado factory, this knife is etched "Havoline Racing." This mint condition lockback knife with famous advertising has a value of $55–65.

Below left: The Chas [Charles] H. Moore Oil Company of Cincinnati, Ohio commissioned Robeson Cutlery Company to produce this unique knife. The knife has three backsprings, each operating a single blade, a rarity among knife styles. In addition to the master blade (unopened), it contains a screwdriver and leather punch, with a patent date of April, 1905. Although the celluloid has shrunk slightly, it is otherwise in near-mint condition. Its value is $125–140.

Below right: This very unique advertising piece could provide the centerpiece of any advertising knife collection. "That Good Oil" is the slogan etched in the yellow celluloid on the rear of the Charles H. Moore Oil Company advertiser. It was photographed against 1930s advertisements for filling station uniforms.

Above: This plastic handled bartender's knife was made as a giveaway for customers who used Shell products. The white plastic sides make the bright red lettering, "Shell Motor Oil," stand out. Cheaply made, these knives are worth only about $10–12. They are, however, a valuable addition for anyone who collects gas station and petroleum items.

Above right: "Monterey Oil Company" commissioned Schrade Walden Cutlery Company to make this two-bladed metal pen knife for the participants of the American Institute of Mining Engineers Convention in 1959. The initials "AIME" are the abbreviations of this group of mining engineers. The value of this knife is $35–40 because of its condition, interesting stamping, and good cutlery manufacturer.

Right: The bright yellow plastic or celluloid on this knife made by Schrade Cutlery provides a background for the "Drake Well Service Company" advertisement. The company was named for the first oil well ever developed, the Drake well. Although the condition of the knife is rough, with some pitting and grind marks, the advertisement is well done and striking. The value of the knife is $30–35, and would be a good addition for someone who collects petroleum collectibles.

Top: Unique mottled blue celluloid provides the background for this unique petroleum advertiser. Although the blades are well-used, the unique bar shield advertising "The Pure Oil Company" make this a worthy find for petroleum collectors. This knife was made by the Stainless Cutlery Company, New York City, a company which was in business from the mid-1920s to the end of the 1930s. Knowing when the cutlery company was in business is valuable in dating the advertisements of companies which are not nationally known. This knife is valued at $25–30, because of its deeply stamped shield, rare blue celluloid handles, and unique advertising. The price would be approximately $10 higher with blades in better condition.

Bottom: This advertiser is unique in that it advertises a British company: "The British American Oil Company, LTD." This cutlery example was made in Sheffield England by J. J. James and Sons, a rare cutlery stamping. The master blade contains what appears to be a cigar cutter located at the tang end of the blade, a unique addition to any knife. Because of extensive wear and broken small blade, this knife has a value of $25, due largely to the unique etched blade advertising.

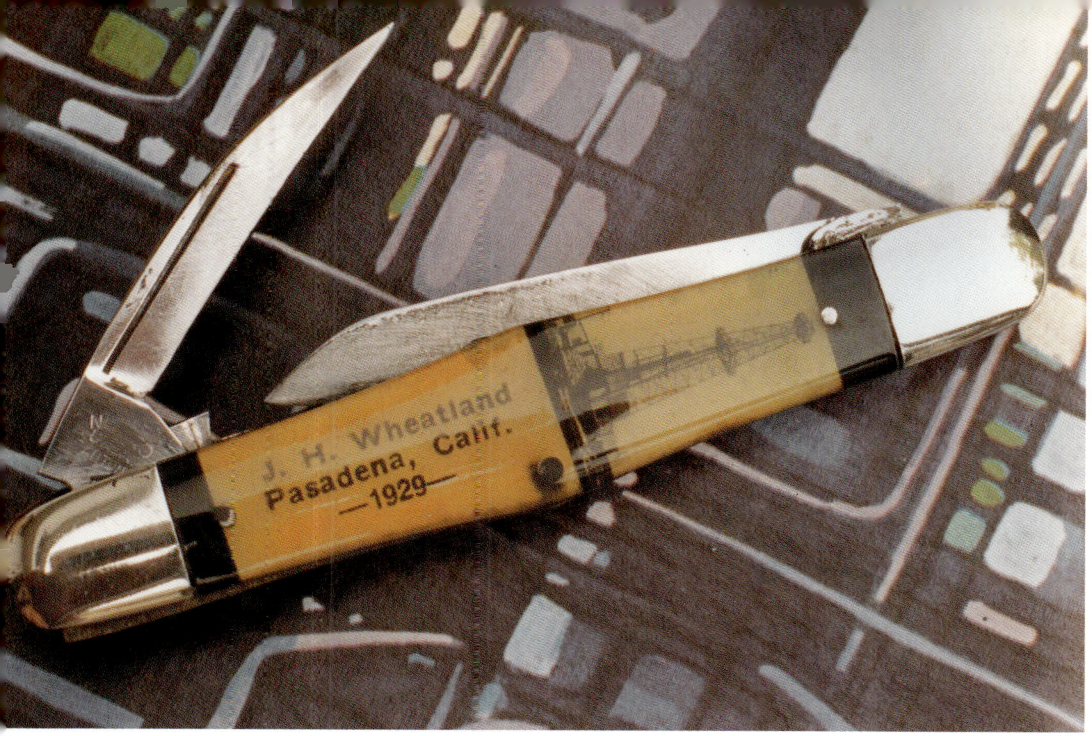

Left: The maker of this unique knife, Canton Cutlery, went out of business in the late 1930s. The rear side of this knife shows an oil derrick and the name of the advertiser, "J. H.. Wheatland, Pasadena, Calif." The inclusion of the date "1929" is an extremely valuable addition. It verifies the production dates of the cutlery manufacturer, and it is an important historical date which corresponds to the beginning of the Great Depression, and the oil boom in California. Although the master blade shows very significant wear, the advertisement stands by itself. The value of this Texaco advertiser would be $50–65 because of the outstanding condition of the celluloid handles and national advertising theme. With full, unsharpened blades, this knife would have a value of $100–120.

Below left: Rarely are examples of national advertising found on the sides of "picture knives" produced by one of only three early cutlery companies. This example, made by the Canton Cutlery Company, encases an advertisement for the Texaco Company. The very well-known "Texaco Star" is placed along with a superb elk photo and a pointing canine retriever. The open blade is a curved "manicure blade," probably a well-used blade in the oil drilling business.

Below right: A closeup of this Texaco advertiser shows the swell center knife style and unique encased photos. Although thousands of these picture knives were produced, most have either cracked or faded throughout the years. This is an outstanding exception.

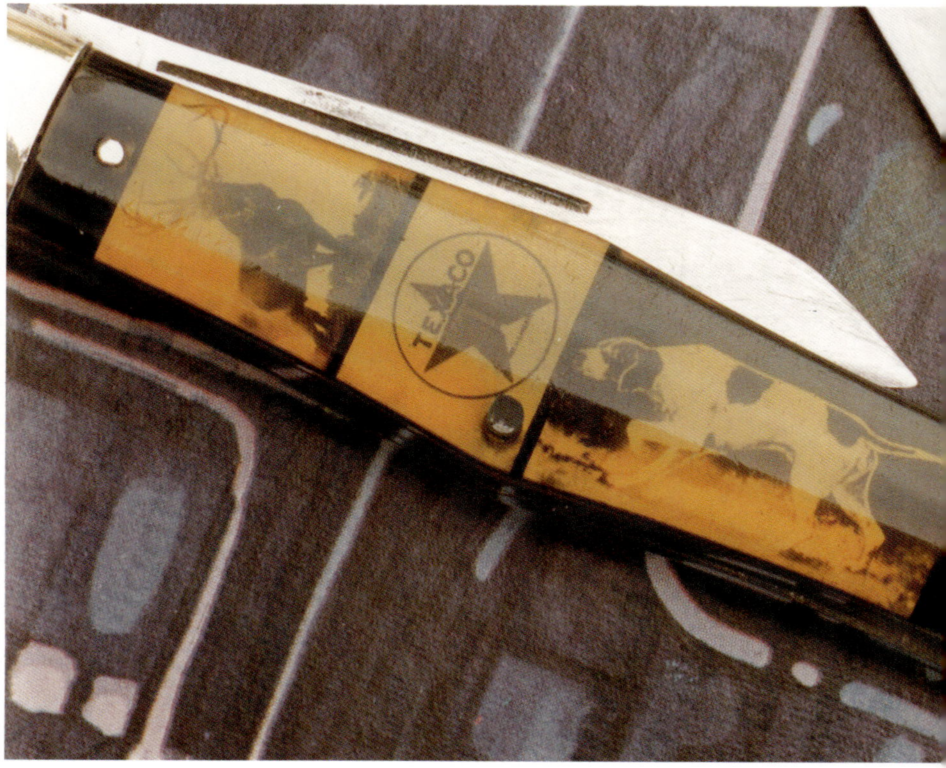

Left: A knife containing a bail on the end almost always indicates a watch fob knife. This metal sided advertiser for the "H. C. Smith Oil Tool Company" was given out to oil company employees in appreciation for purchasing tools associated with the oil drilling industry.The name Compton, California adds to the value of the advertising piece. Value is $25–30.

Below left: Mint advertising knives are always in demand. This example was made by Brit-Nife, a cutlery company located in St. Louis. Using cracked-ice celluloid as a base for the advertisement, the red Texaco star with green lettering is striking. The city where the "Park Service Station" is located is unknown, although we know that the station is located at the corner of "Main and Shaw Street." In this condition, with nationally known Texaco advertising, this knife is worth $35–45.

Below right: This lobster-style knife is a modern advertisement for Texaco. The green and white advertisement makes a striking addition to a collection. Made in Japan, this knife is more valuable to petroleum collectors. Value is $20–25.

VII. FRATERNAL ORGANIZATIONS

This equal end pen with engraved meta sides proclaiming "Flower City Council" was made for use with a pocket watch, thus the attached bail. Closer examination shows a "U. C. T." emblem with a lodge number of #203. This advertiser was most probably a Fraternal Organization which gave knives to members. The tang stamping reads "VOOS," a cutlery firm out of New Haven, Connecticut. VOOS made cutlery as early as 1923. This example probably dates from the 1940s. Fancy engraving and quality craftsmanship help establish a value of $35–45.

Fraternal organizations are not new. In fact, these "secret societies" were popular in the late nineteenth and early twentieth centuries. These societies were formed and founded for many different reasons, but can be classified to fall into the following general groups: military, fraternal, religious, veterans, social, patriotic, political, mystical, and benevolent.

The names of many of these fraternal organizations are common to many of us, and include Free Masonry, Shriners, Knights of Pythias, Knights of Columbus, Order of Odd Fellows, International Order of Foresters, American Legion, Benevolent and Protective Order of Elks, Loyal Order of Moose, and the Veterans of Foreign Wars, to name just a few. Others are less known, and the list of those is quite extensive, numbering about 100 in total.

The oldest and largest of all societies gained popular ground in the British Isles during the early eighteenth century, but actually got its start much earlier. Originally formed as a group of masons and cathedral builders, these workers banded together in lodges, forming a network to provide itinerant workers with a place to live while traveling and working. Since those early days, the society has traveled to the United States from England, Ireland, and Scotland.

For the most part, these fraternal organizations have some common characteristics. They include the stress on moral character, pursuit of intellectual development and knowledge, fellowship and unity through shared beliefs and values, service to those less fortunate, and a respect for religion and higher authority. These beliefs are demonstrated in various rituals and initiations, and show themselves to society in the form of sponsorship of children's hospitals, burn centers, and community service.

Left: This small lobster pen knife was made by an extremely collectible cutlery manufacturer, The Western States Cutlery Company, formerly located in Boulder, Colorado. The handle material is cream and white striped celluloid with the inset shield showing the unique design of a "cross and crown." Research into various fraternal organizations yielded an drawing of the identical shield found on this knife. The shield belongs to the Shrine-Mason organization. All Shriners must become Masons first, and may petition to become a Shriner only after achieving the 32nd degree Scottish Rite. Because it is in mint condition, has very desirable handle material, rare Shrine shield, and an outstanding company stamping, its value would be $70–80 to collectors.

Below left: This equal end pen advertising the K. C. Bill of Fare Press is one of the most unique advertisers, and one of the most confusing. Assuming K.C. stands for Kansas City, this is most probably a newspaper or paper publishing company. It is reasonable to assume, however, that K.C. stands for the "Knights of Columbus," a fraternal organization. If this is the case, this advertiser most probably advertises the Knight's magazine.

Below right: "Tavern Talk" is the advertisement on the back of the K.C. Bill of Fare Press knife. Depending on whether the K.C. stands for Kansas City or Knights of Columbus, the term "Tavern Talk" might refer to a column or section of the newspaper. Value is $30–35.

All of these societies have a rather rigorous system of secret meetings and rituals, often involving specific costumes, greetings, sayings, accessories and such. These rituals often start at the doorway to the lodge where the members exchange certain sayings, knocks, signs, passwords, and handshakes. Like a modern-day college fraternity, initiates are often required to go through some sort of "proving ground" which almost always involves learning certain procedures, songs, tests, and other "ordeals."

The rituals often involve significant readings, meditations, formal initiation ceremonies, symbolic cleansing, prayer, readings, and acceptance ceremony into the fraternity. It is usually a dramatic affair with officers dressed in elaborate costumes, hats, swords, medals, and such. The initiate takes the secret oath, and is taught the various symbolism, mottoes, songs, and passwords.

In general, these fraternities are declining significantly in number. As the older members pass on, their ranks are not being replaced by younger members. In some of these lodges, a member around the age of 50 could be one of the youngest members in the lodge. As a result, many of these societies are openly looking for candidates—in some cases, squeezing all of the required rituals and ranks into a one-day marathon instead of over a period of months or even years.

For the advertising or fraternal collector, this means that those items which are an important part of the initiation and ritualistic rights are held by fewer and fewer people, many of whom are advanced in age. It is now possible to collect cutlery pieces from a variety of these societies in numbers not available a few years ago. In addition, these cutlery examples are from an era which makes them particularly valuable, and are frequently made from outstanding materials, including fancy celluloid handles, sterling silver handles, inlays of various colors and material types. Most of these pieces will be in good condition, since they were not used on a daily basis.

Look for examples which show the various Masonic, Shriner, IOOF, and Odd Fellows symbols in order to identify these pieces. They do truly represent an important part of American (and international) life which is being replaced by a more mobile society.

Above right: This advertiser, which proclaims "Apollinaris" in raised letters, is one of the most interesting knife mysteries. The tang stamping reads "Paul A. Henckels," a German stamping made as early as 1887. Research on the wording turns up some interesting facts. The word Apollinaris was used to describe St. Francis, one of the Saints of the Orthodox Catholic Church. Supposedly, this saint, one of the Bishops of Ravena, was made a bishop by St. Peter himself. Further research indicates that the word "Apollinaris" was used as a trademark for a sparkling mineral water discovered by a German farmer south of Bonn. The spring from which the water came was named for a nearby chapel. This information only partially clears up the mystery connected with this handsome knife. Its unique design, lettering, and quality construction make this cutlery piece worth $80–90.

Right: "Apenta" is the advertisement which appears in raised letters on the sides of this equal end pen knife. The "Fleur-de-lis" pattern on this striking advertiser is one of its outstanding attributes, the other being the striking use of small crosshatching designs used in the lowered portions of the handle background. The "Fleur-de-lis" pattern was widely used on the shields and armor of the Crusaders in Europe. The dramatic lettering stands out boldly because of the darkened background, which is made of very small individual patterned dots. Research on the word "Apenta" turned up no specific company information.

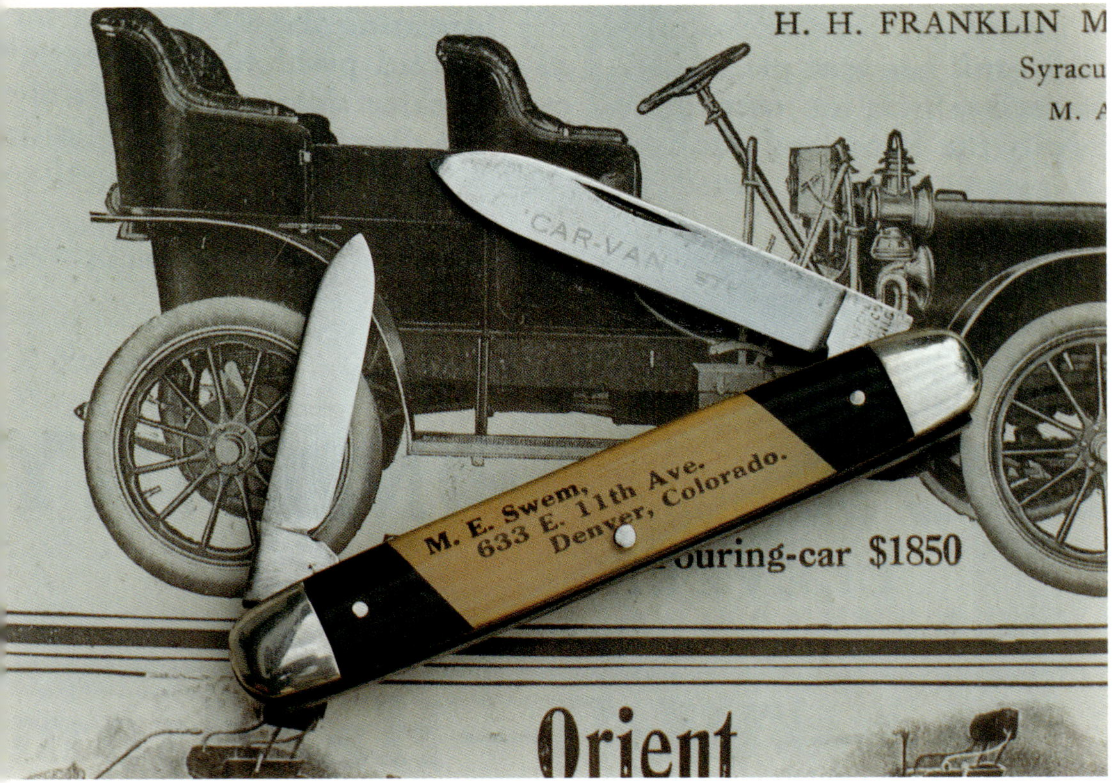

Above left: Because of the numerous cheap imitation Ku Klux Klan knives appearing on the market, it is unique to find an original Klan knife. Made on contract by the New York Knife Company, which went out of business in 1931, this knife can be dated to the 1920s. The handle material on this "senator pen" is an old celluloid called "waterfall," so named because the lines inside of the celluloid appear to actually move when the knife is tilted from side to side like a flowing waterfall. The "advertising" is clear, and was probably given to officers in the K.K.K. Because it is extremely rare, but in very good condition with full blades and extra-sharp colored K.K.K. etching, this knife would be valued at $145–165.

Above right: The closeup photograph shows the "Hammer Brand" tang stamp, a copyrighted stamping owned by the New York Knife Company, until New York Knife went out of business in 1931. The "hammer brand" symbol was then purchased by the Imperial Knife Company to use on their cheaply made knives. The photo also shows a closeup of the K.K.K. engraved insignia. The knife is photographed against an original piece of sheet music entitled "Ku Klux Kismet." Remember, in the 1920s the Ku Klux Klan was, to many cutlery companies, just another contract—much like the Odd Fellows, Woodmen of the World, Masons, and other fraternal organizations.

Left: Canton Cutlery is the maker of this clear celluloid picture knife. This one is personalized with the name of the advertiser; the other side contained one of a variety of scenes from animals, Masonic symbols, nude ladies, family photos, campaign figures, or different forms of transportation. Value depends upon the photo encased in the celluloid, ranging from $20–75, more if presidential candidates are shown on the sides.

Above left: This bartender's knife with caplifter, corkscrew and master blade was produced for the Massachusetts Consistory, a branch of the Masons. The Masons, like other fraternal organizations, have adult lodges, secret initiations, oaths, passwords, and special pins or badges. Most of these organizations stress individual character, fellowship, service to those less fortunate, and religion. Because of the unique symbols associated with the Masonic Order, these knives can be quite valuable. This one is rather plain, but has strong etching and is in mint condition. Its value is $35–45.

Above right: This two-bladed senator pen knife with birdseye rivets was made for the "International Order of Odd Fellows" by the Henry Sears Cutlery Company, which ended production in the late 1950s. The birdseye rivets are used on knives without end bolsters as a way of strengthening the ends of the knife. This knife is unique because it contains not only the I.O.O.F. abbreviations, but also the two famous I.O.O.F. symbols; the linked chain (symbolizing friendship, love, and truth), and the overseeing eye. Although this knife has seen considerable blade wear, the advertising is in good condition. Its value would be $40–50.

Right: Made by the New York Knife Company, this Masonic commemorative knife uses the same birdseye rivets as a way of strengthening the ends of the knife. In addition, the handle material used for this knife is waterfall, an old celluloid which seemed to move like a waterfall when the knife was tilted from side to side. This knife was made before 1931, the year New York Knife went out of business. The value is about $35–45.

Left: This unique enameled pen knife was produced for the Shriner's fraternal organization. The Shriners are the highest order of the Masons. They are most noted for their financial support of the Shriner's hospitals for crippled children and burn victims. Numerous fund raisers support these humanitarian efforts. This particular fraternal knife is unique in the various use of colors illustrating the historic red "fez," its Egyptian origin (illustrated by the pyramid), and the symbolic badge with sword, star, and shield. This knife is a rare find, and is valued at $55–65.

Below left: This swell end pen knife is handled in waterfall celluloid like many of the fraternal knives. This one, however, is stamped with the name of a Kansas hardware store: Blish, Mize, Silliman Hardware, Atchison, Kansas—quite rare for a fraternal knife. The assumption is that this major hardware company ordered knives with the Masonic emblem inset into the knife in place of the regular shield. This knife is in good condition, with full blades and colored Masonic emblem, valued at $40–50.

Below right: Although the blades in this knife have been almost totally destroyed, the Masonic emblems are still strongly etched into the french ivory celluloid handle material. Like many fraternal knives, this example uses birdseye rivets to strengthen the handle material. The value of this knife is limited to about $10 since the blades are unusable.

Above left: The advertisement on this official Victorinox multi-blade knife is "N.R.A.," the initials belonging to the National Rifle Association. Probably given to members or re-subscribers to the National Rifle Organization, this knife is valued at $15–20.

Above right: Voos Cutlery was the producer of this all-metal bartender's knife made for the Fraternal Order of Eagles, Third Lodge. The date of 1930 on the metal sides gives an exact production date. In addition to a master and pen blade, this knife contains a corkscrew and a bail. In mint condition, this knife is worth $35–45 because of its connection to a fraternal organization and its condition.

Left: This small serpentine pen knife advertising Central States is handled in thin yellow celluloid inlaid into a shallow depression in the metal. Cheaply made, its advertisement is intriguing. Ogalala is a city in Nebraska, which is certainly in the "Central States" region. Just what is being advertised is unknown, perhaps some nation-wide business or organization which has broken down into regions. Its value is only $5–10 because of its condition, poor workmanship, and unknown advertisement.

VIII.
WHISKEY & TOBACCO

The Knives of Adolphus Busch

Adolphus Busch migrated to the United States from Germany in 1857. From an already wealthy family, he married Lily Anheuser and joined with her wealthy father in the brewery business. Young Adolphus assisted his father-in-law in turning a mediocre brewery into a multi-million dollar business through aggressive and sometimes questionable business practices. Although he did improve the taste of the brewery's beer, Adolphus also spent a great deal of time purchasing competing breweries or dropping the price of his beer so low that the remaining competition was driven from the market.

The newly formed Anheuser-Busch Company never scrimped on advertising. They promoted new products by advertising heavily in newspapers and magazines, and through giveaways which included serving trays, tip trays, mirrors, clocks, signs, plates, and most importantly, knives.

Sometime around the turn of the century, Adolphus started giving away knives as Christmas gifts. These knives, imported once again from Adolph Kastor, Germany, were given to drivers, salesmen, stable grooms, friends, and acquaintances. Most of these knives were made in a "bartender's" pattern, with four blades. Included were a champagne cork wire cutter, a corkscrew, and two additional blades, for cutting the foil around the top of bottles. Most of these impressive knives were handled in genuine pearl.

This uniquely patterned bartender's knife is crafted in genuine pearl, and proudly advertises the "Anheuser Busch Brewing Company." In addition to two master blades, it contains a corkscrew and champagne bottle wire cutter. These knives were produced around the turn of the century, as advertising giveaways. These knives contain the famous "stanhope" lens located on the side of the knife near one end. By looking through the small lens, the recipient could get a glimpse of Adolphus Busch himself, or a picture of the Anheuser Busch brewing plant. Value with uncracked pearl handles, full blades, and a working stanhope lens is $350–400.

Perhaps the most interesting feature of these knives was the "Stanhope" lens inserted into the handle of the knife. Stanhope lenses were uniquely developed in the field of optics. Because they have an extremely close focusing distance, they can be inserted into very thin spaces. When the viewer held the knife up to his eye, he saw a miniature picture photograph of Adolphus Busch himself, or perhaps a view of the Anheuser-Busch factory. Unfortunately, these Stanhope lens pictures are frequently missing out of the knife, or are sometimes destroyed by the effects of oil on the blades of the knife.

In addition to the pearl Adolphus-Busch knives, there were a wide variety of metal knives made. These knives were made in the same fancy "bartender" shape, but with fancy metal sides, red and black enameling, and fancy scrollwork throughout. Another interesting feature was the gold-gilded blades and the famous Anheuser "A" enameled on the side. Like all other Busch knives, they contained the now-famous Stanhope lens and four blades.

A true find, however, would be to find one of these knives in mint condition in the original engraved leather pouch stating "Compliments of Anheuser-Busch." Many of these metal knives were made by the Schrade-Walden Cutlery Company as late as the 1960s, so examples can still be found today.

Because the Anheuser-Busch knives are uniquely ornate in design, contain the famous "Stanhope" lens, and were made in a variety of styles (some say as many as fifty different styles), they are a fascinating form of advertising. In addition to the fancy "bartender" design, these knives can be found in the shape of a bottle, or in several sizes of equal end pens.

For the collector, champagne or bartender pattern knives can be found with various name stampings in addition to Adolph Kastor, Germany. Among the verified are those which were produced by Wester Bros., Wester and Butz, and A. Graef—all German producers and importers of cutlery products to the United States. Certainly, Anheuser-Busch was not the only company to use these specialty knives to advertise their products. Similar knives were purchased by various producers of wine, champagne, and beer and can be found with the following company imprints: Piper Heidsieck (champagne), Schlitz Beer, Pabst Beer, Pabst Brewing Company, Schmidt and Peters (champagne), and Brut (champagne), to name just a few.

The reverse side of the Anheuser Busch, pearl-handled bartender's knife shows the famous Anheuser "A" with the eagle peering through it. These designs were etched into the pearl handle material and then inked with permanent ink. Finding examples without cracked pearl is a task worth pursuing.

An extreme closeup of the end of the Busch knife shows the intricate Busch "A" worked into the metal bolster. The Anheuser Busch German tang stamp is also clearly seen on the master blade, as is the example of the eagle trademark in the advertisement below the knife. As a collectible, Busch knives make an interesting and quite valuable collection. There are numerous variations of the Anheuser Busch knives available, and some collectors try to find as many as possible.

Above left: In addition to the pearl bartender's knife, the Anheuser Busch Brewing Company commissioned the Schrade Cutlery Company make a unique metal bartender's knife with the same general quality characteristics as their earlier examples. Made in the 1960s, the photograph shows a mint example along with the original leather pouch which contained the knife. The leather pouch, in this condition, with original writing and emblem is itself extremely rare.

Above right: An extreme closeup of the Busch metal knife made by Schrade Walden. The intricate detail of the red, black and gold "cloisonné" design are indications of overall quality. These designs were either color-etched or enameled into the sides of the knife. Like the more rare pearl models, the Schrade Walden Busch knife also contains a stanhope lens encased in the side. Because of the outstanding artwork and design, these knives are true centerpieces of any advertising collection.

Left: In addition to the color-etched sides of this Anheuser Busch knife, the edges and corkscrew were "gold washed." This adds greatly to the overall appearance of this knife, and helps to establish its mint condition. Value in this condition with original leather pouch is $300.

Above left: This is a bartender's or champagne knife because of the corkscrew and wine bottle wire cutter. It is a highly collectible knife style because of its ornate and original design. They were given to liquor stores, night clubs, and restaurants by liquor distributors, in this case "Diplomat Whiskey," whose motto was "just right." Because of its rarity, it would be worth $150–200 in mint condition.

Above right: The reverse side of this Diplomat Whiskey advertiser shows the distributor's name, "Glasner and Barzen, Kansas City." The distributor's location and the fancy scrollwork design also adds to its overall value.

Right: This German knife is also called a bartender's style probably made after the 1920s. Before that time, bartender's knives usually included a champagne bottle wire cutter. "Magnet" was most likely an advertisement for a brand of champagne. This example is handled in two-piece pearl, and contains a corkscrew. Value is based on deep blade etching, superior quality, and intact pearl handles. Value is $85–95.

Top: "Greers O. V. H. Scotch Whisky" is the advertisement proudly etched into the side of this two-bladed metal senator pen. George Ibberson (with the distinctive violin trademark) is the producer of the knife, an English firm which started as early as 1700. With strong etching and desirable product, this knife has a value of $40–50.

Bottom: Bartender's pattern knives were very popular with liquor and wine distributors as advertising giveaways. This knife advertises the "Sunnyside Liquor Company," located, as the knife proclaims, at the corner of 15th and Champa in downtown Denver, Colorado. Included as an accessory are a cigar cutter built into the body, as well as a champagne corkscrew. Over the years, the metal plating has chipped off of the bartender's knife, most noticeably around the lettering. In spite of this defect, this knife is worth from $65–75 because of its unique style, age, and strong engraving.

Above: This two-bladed pen knife advertises "Wee Mc Kay Liquors," not only on both sides of the handles but also on the blade itself. Gin, whiskey, and scotch are all advertised. Unique because of its three-panel celluloid sides, this Pal brand knife was imported into the United States from either Germany or Czechoslovakia during the late 1920s to 1930s. Its value would be $45–55.

Above right: The rear side of the "Wee Mc Kay Liquor" advertiser contains a second advertisement for "U. D. L. Old Canadian Rye." This knife would have been given out to liquor store owners or bar owners by wholesale liquor distributors.

Right: This ornately designed metal-handled knife was made for "Storz" Beer. Although of fairly recent production, this advertising knife was made by the German firm of Giesen and Forsthoff. In pristine condition, this knife is supremely crafted, with intricate engraving. Normally, beer advertisers are not of this quality. This knife is valued at $45–55 because of its mint condition.

A unique pair of "Storz" Beer advertisers. One is a traditional two-bladed pen knife, and the second a well-designed three-blade with fingernail file in the back. Notice the difference in the metal engraving patterns on the sides of both knives. Both are in pristine mint condition. The value of the pair could run as high as $100–120.

Left: Advertising knives with unique shapes are always worth picking up. This cylindrical two-bladed keychain knife advertises the "Southwest Missouri Liquor Company." With both red and cracked-ice celluloid, it is a striking example of advertising.

Below: A second photograph of the cylinder liquor advertiser shows the various specialties, phone number, and location. With a phone number of "1196" you know this knife was made in the 1930s. The location of Southwest Missouri Liquor Company was Joplin, Missouri. Because of its unique design, use of color and age, its value is $40–50.

Above left: A bartender's style with tip bolsters, corkscrew, and cap lifter are included in this "Doom Benedictine" liquor advertiser. Although the knife is in good condition, some of the etching is worn off.

Above right: This particular advertiser, produced by Camillus Cutlery, using the "Kent" tang stamping, was commissioned by the "Julius Wile Sons & Co, Inc., New York." The Kent stamping dates this knife to the 1930s as Kent was made specifically for the F. W. Woolworth's Department Store in 1934. Obviously, the stamping was used for other commissions besides Woolworth's. The value would be $15–20.

Right: A genuine Victorinox two-bladed knife is used to advertise the "Adolph Coors Company" of Golden, Colorado. These small knives are well-made, with the known Victorinox quality, and well-received by customers and collectors. Unlike most Victorinox knives, which are plastic, this one is metal-handled with enameled paint and engraving. Its value would be $15–20.

Left: The Budweiser Clydesdale draft horses are the subject of this commemorative knife made by the Utica Cutlery Company. Bearing the Kutmaster stamping, this knife has well-designed metal sides depicting these famous horses, which are used to pull the Budweiser beer wagons. These horses, some of which are housed and bred at Sea World in San Diego, are always a hit with children and grownups alike.

Below left: A closeup photograph shows the portraits of two Clydesdales, which are, as the knife states, "world famous." Fancy scrollwork and leaf palms add to the design. The value of this mint commemorative would be $40–50.

Below right: The back panel of the Budweiser knife shows a farm or ranch scene which includes a child brushing a horse, baby foal with mother, and horse caretaker. The scenes are well executed, and make for a handsome cutlery piece.

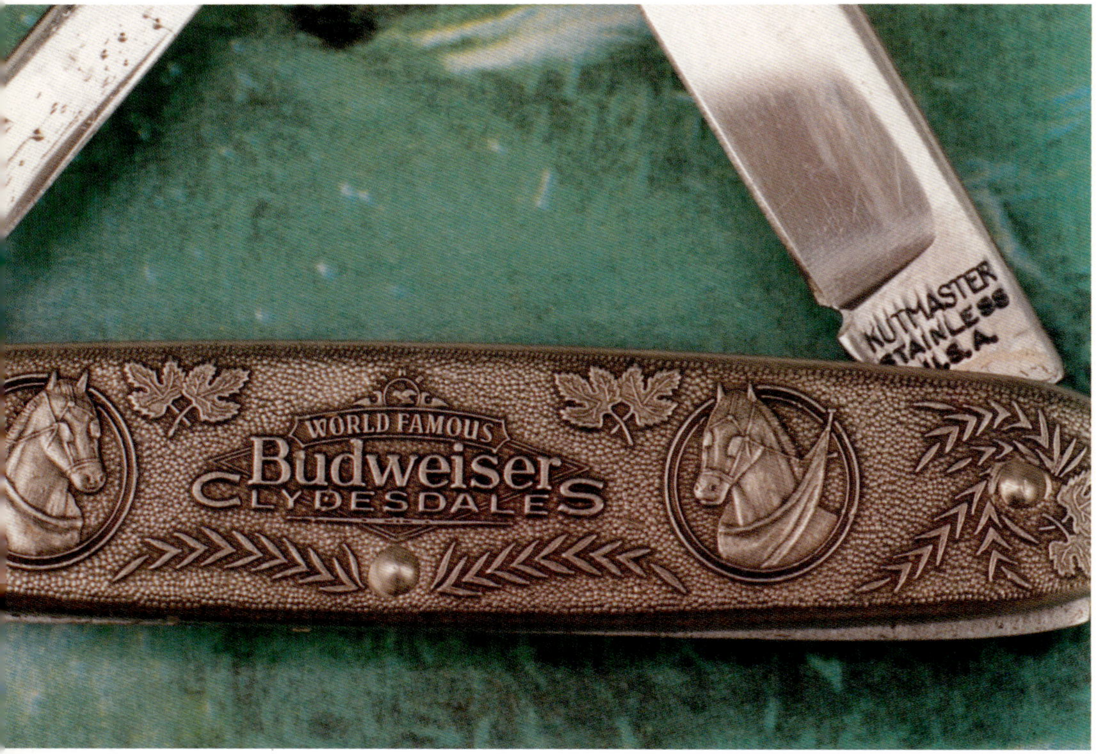

This Prince Albert tin would not be included in a book dealing with advertising cutlery were it not for the ad on the back. Notice, however, the original price for the tobacco tin at 18 cents. This tin dates from the late 1950s, early 1960s.

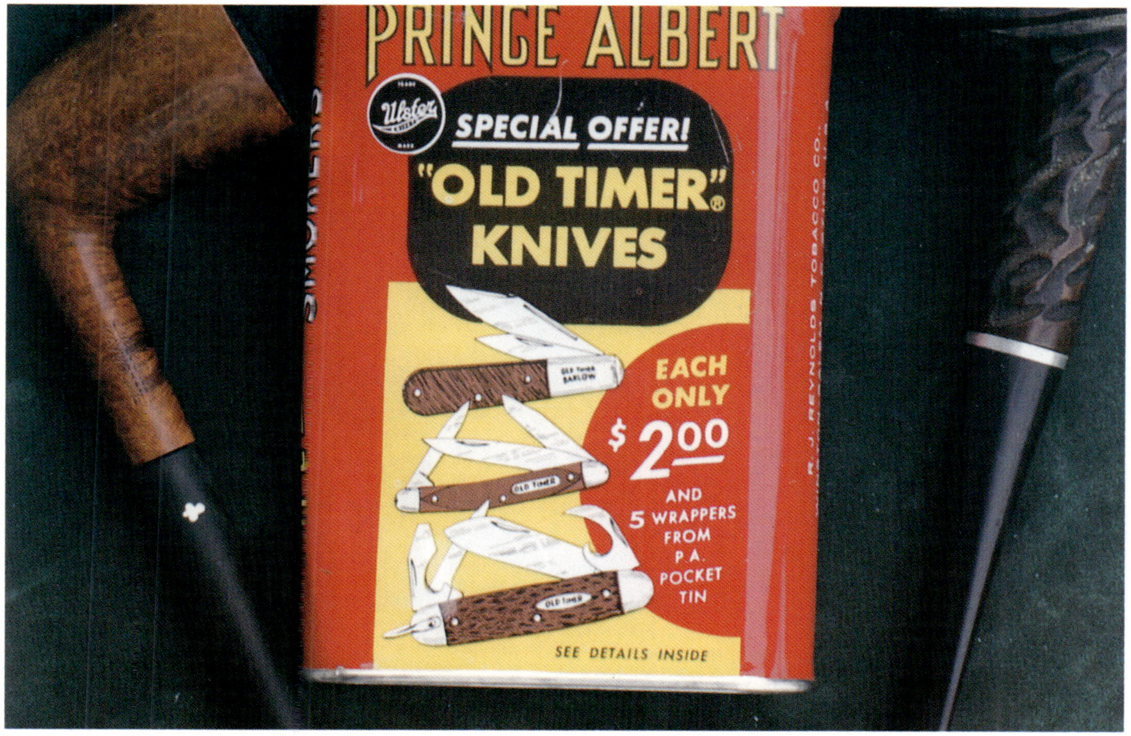

The rear of this Prince Albert can is of special interest to knife collectors. The advertisement features a special offer of three knives which were available to customers for "$2.00 and five labels from a pocket tin." Dedicated knife collectors have purchased this tin, and then have searched for the three knives featured on the back. The knives featured on the tin are (top to bottom) barlow, small three-bladed stockman, and a scout-utility four-bladed pattern. The value of the tin is $15–20 in outstanding condition. A set of these three knives in mint condition, along with the tin, was priced at over $100 at a recent antique show.

Above left: This unique cigar advertising knife was most likely made during the 1920s, but the cutlery company is unknown. A recently discovered "Y. B." cigar box provided the following information. This knife was made available to smokers who purchased ten Y. B. (Yokum Brothers) cigars. By sending in a certificate that had been enclosed in the cigar box, you would receive a knife with your name engraved on it. Y. B. cigar knives are rare, and are the only example of tobacco advertising stamped into the blade tang. Y. B. Cigars were located in Reading, Pennsylvania. Value is $40.

Above right: A closeup photograph showing the "Y. B. Cigar" stamping on the tang of the knife. Apparently, customers could order this knife and have their name engraved on the side of the knife by the Y.B. Cigar Company.

Left: This advertising knife made for the "Brecht" Company is called a "cigar cutter." It is used to snip off the ends of a cigar. Smoking collectibles are increasing in value rapidly as more laws are passed regarding smoking in public places, and the health lawsuits are being settled. This knife is valued at $25.

Top: This Schrade Cutlery-produced knife advertising "Copenhagen" is of recent production. It contains not only a Copenhagen (smokeless chewing tobacco) shield set in the plastic handles, but is also etched on the master blade. Although recently produced, the increased legislative pressure on tobacco products may make this knife a good collectible. Present value is $20–25.

Bottom: Of very recent Chinese production, this two-bladed knife contains one locking blade and advertises "Skoal" on the bolster. Given as an incentive knife to those who use this smokeless tobacco, it is a well-made knife. Bearing no significant cutlery stamping, its value is $15–20.

IX.

COMMEMORATIVES & ANNIVERSARIES

Above: Made as an almost duplicate of the original Lone Ranger knife, this recent advertiser commemorates the 60th Anniversary of the formation of the Lone Ranger, as indicated on the etched blade. Without this etching, this knife might be mistaken for the 1940s-1950s original which sells in the $65–75 range. Even the "Camco" tang stamping is like the original. Camco was Camillus Cutlery's cheaper brand name. Value of this commemorative, which was also produced in black and red, is $15–20.

Left: This knife is a replica of the original 1936 knife made by F. R. Olbertz, Solingen Germany—a manufacturer which started making knives in 1915. Handled in "gunmetal" with striking inlay, this three-bladed knife commemorates the original launching of the "Hindenburg" at the 1936 Olympics in Berlin, Germany. Mystery still surrounds the crash of this most famous Zeppelin on May 6, 1937 in Lakehurst, New Jersey. Because it is in mint, unused condition, and contains outstanding inlays, it is valued at $55.

Left: Centennial anniversary pieces are, in the opinion of some collectors, sure to appreciate in value. This one celebrates the 100th anniversary of the "Sierra Club." Made as a lockback, using engraved brass handles, this knife is quite well-made.

Below: Made in the U.S.A. by United Cutlery, this knife has stainless blades. The Sierra Club motto engraved on the back of the knife is depicted in raised letters. Because it advertises a centennial, its production year is easy to determine—1992. Value is $30–35, certainly higher to environmentalists.

Right: Because 1986 was the 100th anniversary of the erection of the Statue of Liberty, this year saw the proliferation of numerous commemorative knives with the Statue of Liberty as its theme. This particular example is one of the best, a lockback made by Buck.

Far right: The motto "Keep the Torch Lit" was one of many themes attached to this Statue of Liberty anniversary knife. Many were produced to raise money for the restoration and replateing of the Statue of Liberty. This example, because of its famous symbol, well-known cutlery trademark, and lockback style is valued at $40–50.

Above: John Primble, Belnap Hardware is the producer of this equal end pen knife handled in brass with raised "Statue of Liberty." This example is in mint condition, and proclaims its production date clearly as 1986.

Above right: The rear of this brass-handled commemorative knife displays the words written on the base of the Statue of Liberty. "Give me your tired, your poor..." A collection of Statue of Liberty paraphernalia, including knives, would contain literally hundreds of objects. Value of this example is determined by the mint condition, raised letters, and ever-popular subject. Value is $40–50.

Right: Schrade Cutlery produced this Liberty Bell Commemorative for the consumer market. The shield is a replica of the famous Liberty Bell and the master blade is inscribed "Liberty." The knife model is a small, three-blade stockman with black delrin handles. As an overall collectible, it lacks a flashy shield, expensive handle material or color etching—all characteristics which would give it real value. Value is $25.

Right: Parker Cutlery is the maker of this Statue of Liberty commemorative razor knife. This knife was produced for the Statue of Liberty centennial in 1986. In mint condition, it is valued at $25–30.

Below left: Appealing generally to those involved in hunting, this brass-handled lockback, filled with a variety of hunting animals and scenes—all appropriate to the hunting theme—decorate the front of a Remington Commemorative. It is of recent vintage, circa 1990s, and is valued at $30–40.

Below right: The rear of the Remington lockback commemorative tells its purpose. This knife celebrates "America's Oldest Gunmaker: Remington—Since 1816." Original knives made during the 1930s by Remington are extremely collectible and valuable in good condition. These recent commemoratives, although well made, are probably not going to appreciate significantly in value in the near future.

Above: The brass handles of this mint jack knife tell the whole story. This knife commemorates the "144th Anniversary of Smith and Wesson," a name well-known to gun enthusiasts.

Above right: Ornately detailed, with a picture of the founder, Mr. Horace Smith, as well as examples of an S&W repeating pistol, the reverse side of the Smith and Wesson commemorative shows the same intricate detailing. Because of the mint condition and popular subject matter, this knife has a value of $25–30, in part due to the cheaper construction—using rivets to assemble the knife instead of pins.

Right: W. R. Case Cutlery Company produced this commemorative knife for Ducks Unlimited. Probably given with a donation to this non-profit company, it features both a duck-head shield and blade etching. Although this equal end pen is handled in wood, its value would be limited to those interested in this particular organization. Since W. R. Case is a very well-known knife brand, its value would be approximately $30–35.

Collectors know the Winchester name. This reproduction commemorative lockback is handled in brass with raised letters. Very well-made, the Winchester name is stamped into the blade. Because it is of recent production, in the early 1990s, it would not appreciate significantly in value in the near future. Value is $30.

Bridge Cutlery, located in St. Louis, was the producer of this baseball advertising bat knife. Bridge Cutlery made knives from about 1900 to about 1931. This information helps date this special knife. Embedded in the end of the knife is a baseball, engraved with the words "National League Ball." Bat figurals are always valuable and very collectible, especially in good condition. This one is handled in mottled brown celluloid, and is valued at $75–85.

Above : This lockback was issued by an automobile parts company, the Hastings Company. Made by W. R. Case Cutlery Company of Bradford, PA., it is collectible because of its maker and the fact that it is a lockback knife. For beginning knife collectors, the W. R. Case Cutlery Company is quite unique. Case uses a system of symbols and dots which tell the purchaser when the knife was produced. Using this system, a collector can examine a particular knife, and by viewing the system of dots on the tang portion of the master blade, tell the production date. This information is very valuable in determining the age of a particular pocketknife. In addition, Case knives are perhaps the most documented cutlery brand, appearing in several outstanding publications. These publications outline the values of knives made during the nearly 100 years that Case has been in production.

Above right: The reason for issuance of this knife is clearly stated: 75th Anniversary of the automobile assembly line, in 1912. Adding 75 years to 1912 gives a production date of 1987, a sure way to arrive at the knife production date. This knife, in mint condition, is valued at $35–40.

This official Victorinox two-bladed knife commemorates Longine's participation in the 1976 Winter Olympics in Innsbruck, Austria. The Longine's Company was, as indicated in the advertisement, the "official timer" of this famous Winter Olympics. Unique about this particular advertiser is the second or small blade. Instead of having a normal pen blade, this knife was produced with a special "watch case" blade. Shorter and sturdier than a normal blade, with a narrowed but not sharpened cutting edge, this knife is unique because of this feature. Value would be $20–25.

Above: Knives are produced to commemorate a multitude of events. This three-bladed whittler pattern was made by Boker in 1975 to commemorate the development of the sternwheeler steamboat. With the shield made in the shape of a steamboat, mint condition, original packaging, and etched blade, this knife is worth $50–60.

Above right: The etching on the front of this knife clearly shows the advertiser of this giveaway as "Traffic Club of Denver, Colorado." Handled in cracked-ice celluloid, this knife features a "matchstriker" pull on the main blade and mint condition. Value is $50–60 because of condition, presence of actual date issued, and Western Cutlery stamping.

Right: This advertising pen knife was given away during the "1961 Colorado Transportation Day." The year marking greatly assists in determining the date of production. The #261 on the master blade is the production number for this style of knife.

Above: Queen Cutlery was the producer of this knife commemorating the first oil well dug in the United States. Colonel Edwin Drake drilled this first well in 1859. Queen Cutlery Company is appropriately located in Titusville, Pennsylvania, the site of this first oil well. Queen produces outstanding bone-handled knives, and this Barlow is no exception. In addition to the engraved master blade, this knife has the Queen logo stamped into the front bolster.

Above right: A closeup of the Queen Cutlery commemorative shows the picture of the "Drake" oil well derrick and adjoining building. The value of this knife in mint condition would be $45–55.

Right: Produced in the 1980s, this reproduction of the famous Remington "Bullet" knife (originals sell in the $1000 range), was purchased as a commemorative of a Secret Service pistol match. Because of its recent production date, and the fact that the handle material is "delrin" (modern plastic), its value is in the $40 range, perhaps as much as $50 to those specifically interested in the actual shooting event.

Right: This pair of interesting knives made in the equal end pen style commemorate the 1980 presidential campaign. Made by W. R. Case and Company, a very famous and quite collectible cutlery company, these knives are in mint condition. In addition to the date engraved on the sides, W. R. Case has a comprehensive dating system well-known to Case collectors. Case uses a series of dots and symbols etched into the tang portion of the master blade. Because of this dating system, novice collectors can accurately discern the production date of all Case knives, a significant advantage to collectors.

Below left: The Democratic presidential knife is decorated with Jimmy Carter's name, the Democratic symbol—a donkey, and the year 1980. It has a value of $40–50.

Below right: The Republican presidential knife is decorated with the name of the Republican presidential candidate, Ronald Reagan; the Republican symbol, the elephant; and the year 1980. Its value is also $40–50 in mint condition. Not only do these knives appeal to Case cutlery collectors and advertising collectors, but they find a ready market in the political collectibles market. In this market, these knives would be valued perhaps as high as $120 for the pair.

X. WORLD'S FAIRS & SOUVENIRS

A world's fair in the middle of the Great Depression was a significant event. This commemorative knife is an original from the 1933-34 Chicago World's Fair. The front commemorates the "Federal Building," a stylized skyscraper, complete with statue. Made by NShure Cutlery Company of Chicago, it is handled in brass. Because of its original condition, age, and rarity, it is of significant collector value. Value is $80–90. Because it is handled in brass, it remains in very good condition. Since there are collectors who specialize in World's Fair memorabilia, this price may go as high as $100–115.

The back panel of this 1933-34 Chicago World's Fair knife shows a raised "art deco" style building housing what was called the "Hall of Science," complete with towers and spotlight shadow. These specifically designed buildings, built with the latest technological and artistic features, must have looked extremely "futuristic" to the thousands of visitors during this Great Depression era.

A second company to produce a Chicago World's Fair model was the Imperial Knife Company. This example, in mint condition, features Fort Dearborn. This knife was produced with no bolsters, usually common on pen knives. The reason, perhaps, was to allow a larger picture to be shown under the clear celluloid handles. The enclosed picture features the famous landmark of Fort Dearborn near Chicago, featured because it was founded 100 years before this Fair in 1833.

A Century of Progress" was the theme of this 1933 Chicago World's Fair. The Chicago skyline is featured on the back of this unusual Imperial pen knife. Because of its mint, unsharpened condition, the famous fair it commemorates, and its unique use of sepia pictures, it is valued at $60–70.

Left: An interesting commemorative for the 1933 World's Fair in Chicago was made by the Hibbard, Spencer, and Bartlett company of Chicago. Handled in cracked-ice celluloid with bold engraving, this knife is over sixty-five years old. Given its historical significance, full blades, and outstanding condition, it is worth $60–75.

Below: Hibbard, Spencer, and Bartlett proudly displayed their company name on the reverse of this World's Fair Commemorative knife. This company was the forerunner of the Tru-Value Hardware giant that began in Chicago and spread throughout the United States.

Top: The 1982 Knoxville World's Fair was the subject of this commemorative knife made by Parker Cutlery Company. The scenes on this metal-sided knife are neatly done, and fifteen years have passed since this knife was produced. Unfortunately, thousands of these knives were produced, and mint examples in the box can still be found. Because of this factor, the value in mint condition is $20–25.

Bottom: Featuring the Space Shuttle *Columbia*, along with Davey Crockett and Daniel Boone, adds value to this commemorative. This knife is probably one which will appreciate in time, as it was originally distributed primarily in the southern United States.

Top: In addition to being produced in silver material, the 1982 Knoxville World's Fair commemorative knives were produced with brass sides. Value for these knives is the same as those produced with metallic sides, $20–25.

Bottom: This knife is strictly an advertising souvenir, made for sale in Washington D.C. Cheaply made with brass sides, it nevertheless shows good engraving, and commemorates the U.S. Capitol and White House. Because it was made by mass production knife companies, and doesn't advertise a particular product, the value is $10.

This small goldstone celluloid equal end pen knife was an obvious souvenir knife made by the famous Western States Cutlery Company, Boulder, Colorado. An actual photograph of the Denver skyline provides the background for this small knife. As an advertiser its value is based on strong lettering, very desirable handle material, and strongly collected cutlery stamping. This knife was made during the 1940s, and is valued at $30–40. The wear on the blades detracts somewhat from the overall price.

These diminutive knives, only about 1 ½" in length, were made by the thousands for sale to tourists. They date to the 1950s, and make an interesting collection. Value is about $5–7, depending on the product advertised. The "flip knife" advertising, "Homer R. Dolin," is a rare style, and is valued at $10–15.

Top: These miniature "Easy-open" jack knives are truly unique because of the quality workmanship found in them. The center knife advertises "CARLSBAD," a reference to Carlsbad Caverns in New Mexico. These were obviously a tourist item, complete with bail for attaching them to a watch chain.

Bottom: This macro photograph shows the small size of this knife to be only two inches in length. Made by Imperial Knife Company in the 1920s and early 1930s, they feature solid nickel silver bolsters, and real celluloid handles. Look for the pins holding the celluloid handles on the knife sides to determine if the knife is of high quality. Value ranges from $15–20, more if advertising is stamped into the knife.

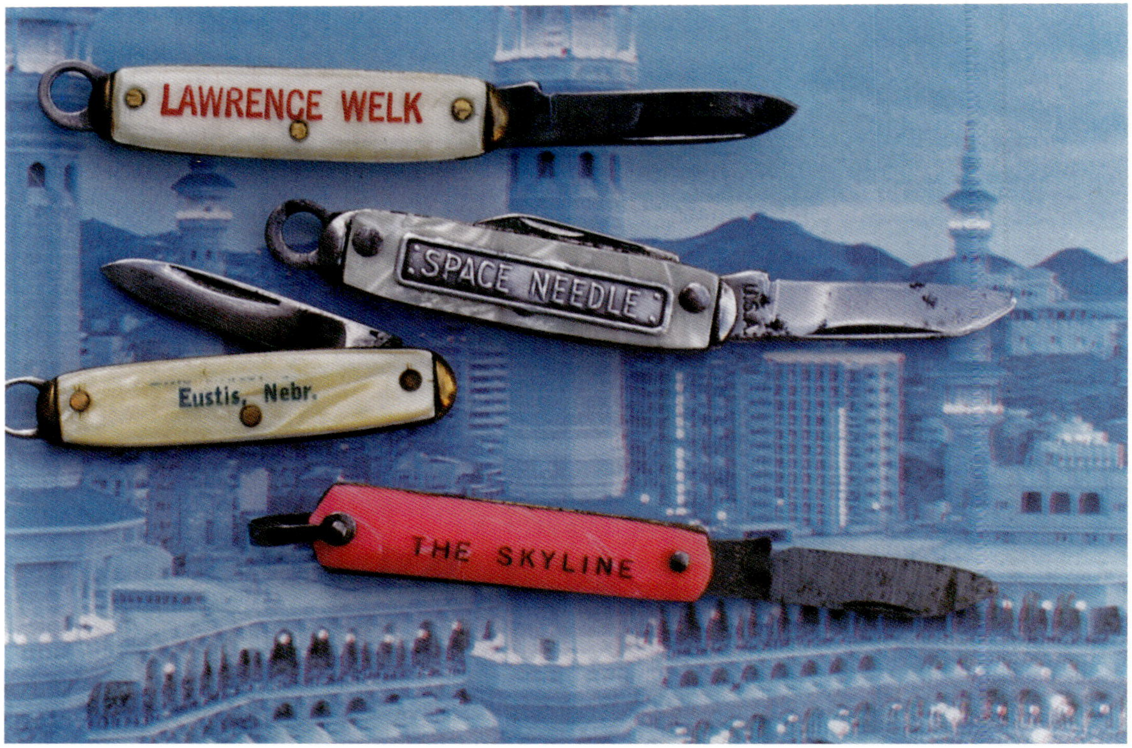

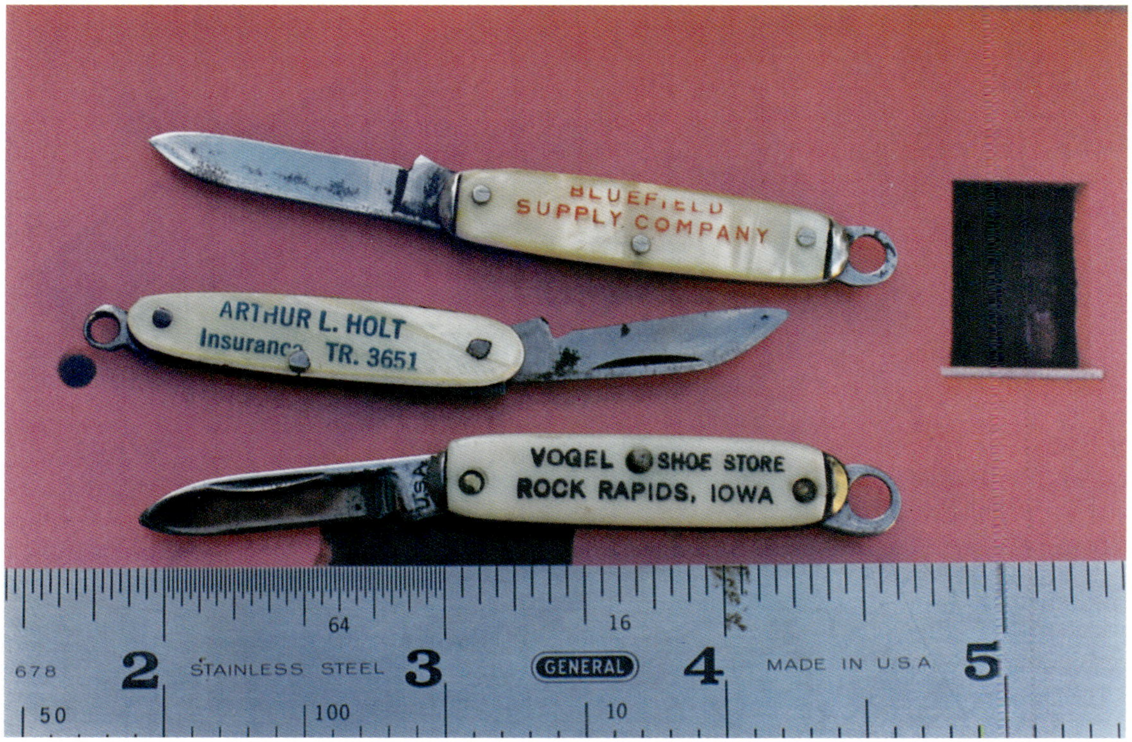

Top: A dozen of these miniatures would fit into the palm of your hand. Keychain knives would be interesting to collect. Some advertise famous sites, others reasonably obscure towns. Most date from the late 1950s or early 1960s.

Bottom: Who ever heard of Bluefield or Rock Rapids? All of these miniatures were made as "giveaways" to customers. They were a favorite of kids in the 1950s. Since most were cheaply constructed, value is $5–7 each.

Left: Normally, sheath knives are not used for advertising purposes, however, this outstanding example stamped "Deer Ridge" was made by the Western Cutlery Company, Boulder, Colorado, in the 1940s or before. It is very small for a sheath knife, only about six inches including the handle, but is made in the hunting style with upswept blade and serrated thumb grove on the upper side of the blade. "Deer Ridge" is engraved on the cracked-ice celluloid handle, but its exact location is unknown. Because of unique size, mint condition, original sheath etched "Western," and deeply etched, unique advertising, its value is $65–75.

Below left: A second example of a small sheath knife made by the Western Cutlery Company of Boulder, Colorado. This knife advertises the famous "Catalina Island" in California, and was probably sold in the 1950s in California souvenir shops. This model is tang stamped "West Cut," Western's lower-quality cutlery line, but this knife is still a quality piece. The brand name, original sheath, and strong stamping would make this knife worth $55–65.

Below right: This multi-bladed utility knife is a copy of the famous Victorinox knives. Made to sell at Yellowstone National Park, it is of recent production, made by Colonial Cutlery Company, probably as late as the 1970s to the mid 1980s. Value is $10–20.

Top: Produced mainly as souvenirs, these inexpensively made, colorful knives were sold at "Smokey Mountain Knife Works" store in Sevierville, Tennessee. Although colorful, these knives are certainly not collector pieces, and are valued at $10.

Bottom: These knives are examples of recent advertising reproductions for such famous companies as Harley-Davidson and Coca-Cola. Made by a variety of different companies, often imported from China or Pakistan, and classified as "novelty items." Often sold as souvenirs, their value is $5–10 each.

Left: An interesting all-metal souvenir knife made for Yellowstone National Park. The words "Yellowstone Park" are formed as if they were sticks of wood laid on the ground. Although this knife contains no maker's name on the tang, it is well made. Value is $20–30.

Right: The rear panel of the Yellowstone Park Souvenir knife portrays three of its most famous tourist attractions: Great Falls of the Yellowstone, twin (bear) cubs, and Old Faithful Geyser. An interesting knife, probably made in the 1950s.

XI. CUTLERY PRODUCTS

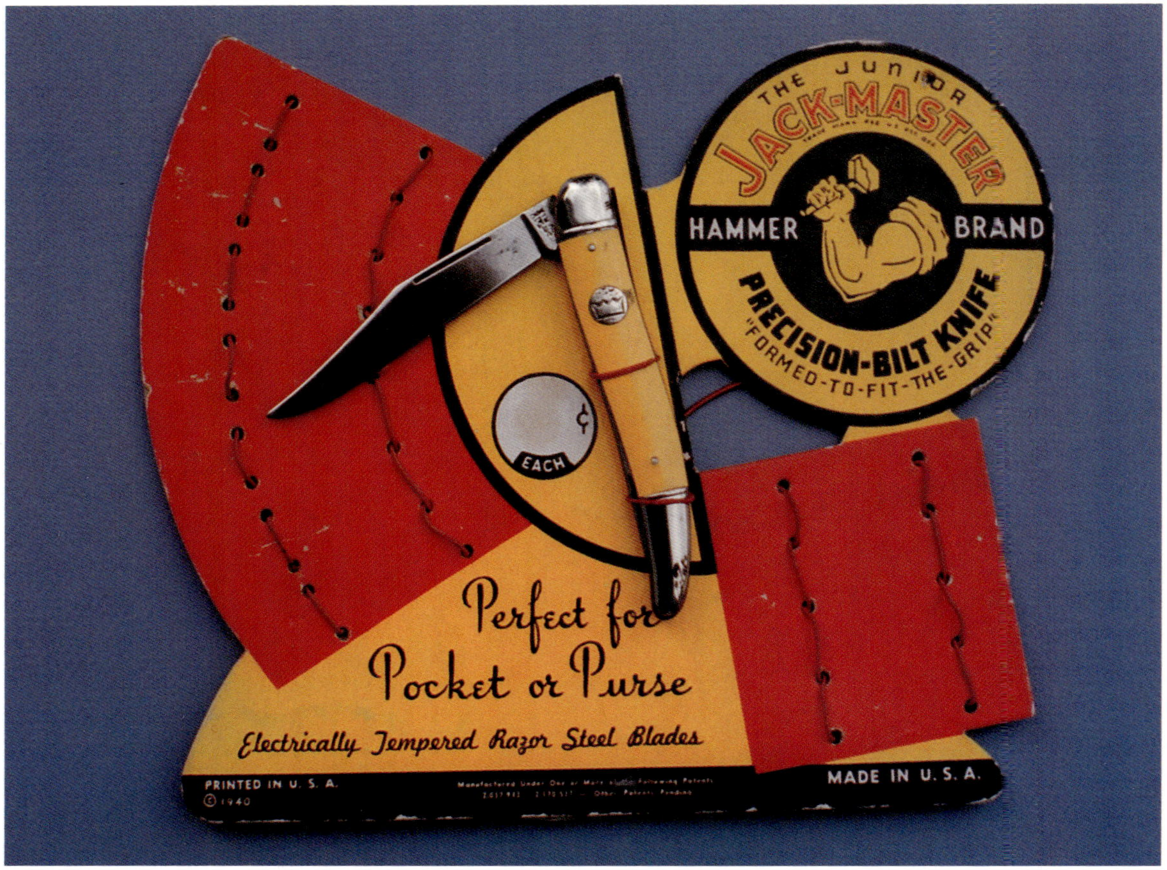

This unique knife advertisement is called a "standing knife card." One dozen cheaply-made jack knives were fastened under the elastic bands which ran around the card. The striking color drew attention to this card which had fold-up cardboard "legs" on the back. These cards were placed on countertops or showcase tops in the 1950s and 1960s. Value in mint condition is $25–35.

Top: This particular miniature is interesting to knife collectors because it advertises a knife brand, Camillus Cutlery Company. The Camillus slogan, "Camillus Has The Edge," is engraved on the side. To a knife collector, this advertiser would be worth $10–15.

Bottom: A second advertisement for the Camillus Cutlery Company. "Camillus Has The Edge" was obviously a common slogan, with the word "edge" being used as a double meaning—competitive edge and knife's sharp edge. Knives shaped like keys are especially popular and rarely in good condition. This one would be worth $25–30.

Left: This large countertop showcase was made and distributed by Camillus Cutlery Company. The advertisement on the side reads: "First Choice for Fine Knives." The top and bottom of the showcase also extol the virtues of Camillus Cutlery. Cutlery Showcases provided constant advertising for their products, just sitting on a glass countertop. For the cutlery collector, original cutlery showcases are just the thing to bring out the best in their collection. Value is $125–150.

Below: This display card was found attached to the inside of the door of a Camillus showcase. The helpful tips and suggestions were designed to help the dealer sell more knives, by explaining how "Camillus has the Edge." Suggestions included oiling the knives at the joints and keeping the showcase glass clean.

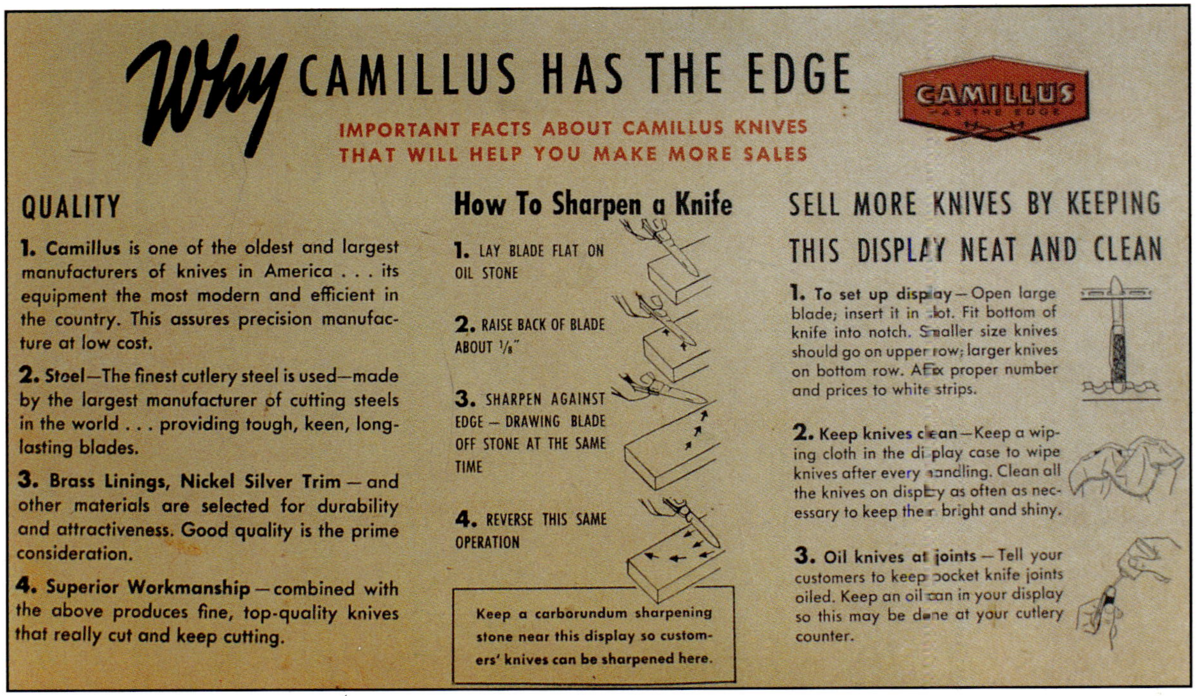

Why CAMILLUS HAS THE EDGE

CAMILLUS HAS THE EDGE

IMPORTANT FACTS ABOUT CAMILLUS KNIVES THAT WILL HELP YOU MAKE MORE SALES

QUALITY

1. **Camillus** is one of the oldest and largest manufacturers of knives in America . . . its equipment the most modern and efficient in the country. This assures precision manufacture at low cost.

2. **Steel**—The finest cutlery steel is used—made by the largest manufacturer of cutting steels in the world . . . providing tough, keen, long-lasting blades.

3. **Brass Linings, Nickel Silver Trim** — and other materials are selected for durability and attractiveness. Good quality is the prime consideration.

4. **Superior Workmanship** — combined with the above produces fine, top-quality knives that really cut and keep cutting.

How To Sharpen a Knife

1. LAY BLADE FLAT ON OIL STONE

2. RAISE BACK OF BLADE ABOUT 1/8"

3. SHARPEN AGAINST EDGE — DRAWING BLADE OFF STONE AT THE SAME TIME

4. REVERSE THIS SAME OPERATION

Keep a carborundum sharpening stone near this display so customers' knives can be sharpened here.

SELL MORE KNIVES BY KEEPING THIS DISPLAY NEAT AND CLEAN

1. **To set up display** — Open large blade; insert it in slot. Fit bottom of knife into notch. Smaller size knives should go on upper row; larger knives on bottom row. Affix proper number and prices to white strips.

2. **Keep knives clean** — Keep a wiping cloth in the display case to wipe knives after every handling. Clean all the knives on display as often as necessary to keep them bright and shiny.

3. **Oil knives at joints** — Tell your customers to keep pocket knife joints oiled. Keep an oil can in your display so this may be done at your cutlery counter.

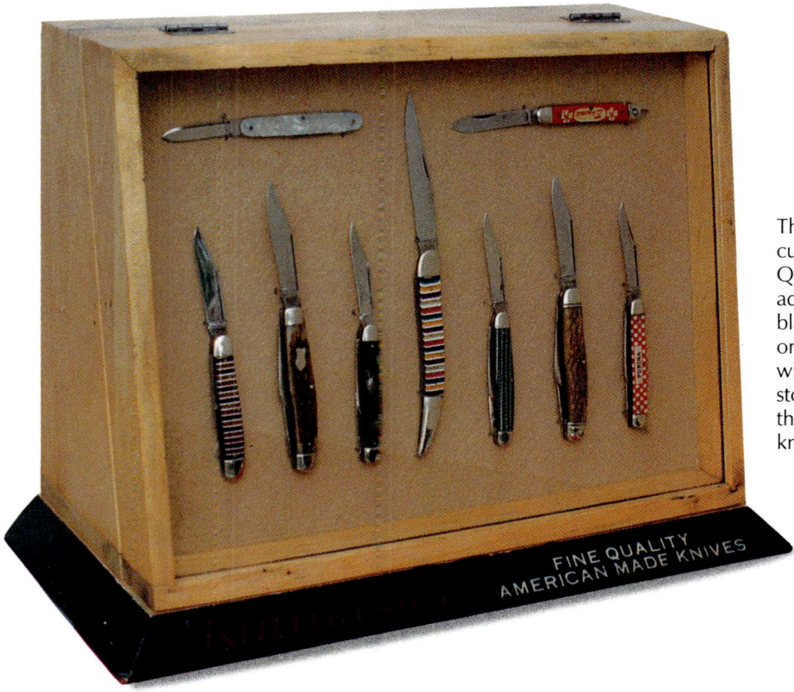

This rare wooden display case was itself a cutlery advertisement. "Kutmaster, Fine Quality American Made Knives" is the advertisement painted on the front of the black bottom panel. These showcases sat on countertops in hardware stores, filled with Kutmaster knives. Extra stock was stored in the various drawers located in the back of the showcase. Value without knives is $90–125.

"World's Finest Pocketknives" is the advertising slogan found on the side of this wooden Schrade Walden cutlery showcase. The white panel below the knives shows the prices as ranging from $2–4.50—an indication of the age of the showcase. The Schrade Walden stamping was used from 1946 to the 1950s. Value is based on solid wood construction, intact lettering, and original pricing marks. Value $125–150.

This small, unique countertop showcase is filled with Western Cutlery pocketknives, known to collectors as the "Western Boulder" stamping. The original prices are below each knife, and range from $2–5. This dates this showcase to the 1950s. This showcase is unique because of its small size and good condition. It is valued at $100–125.

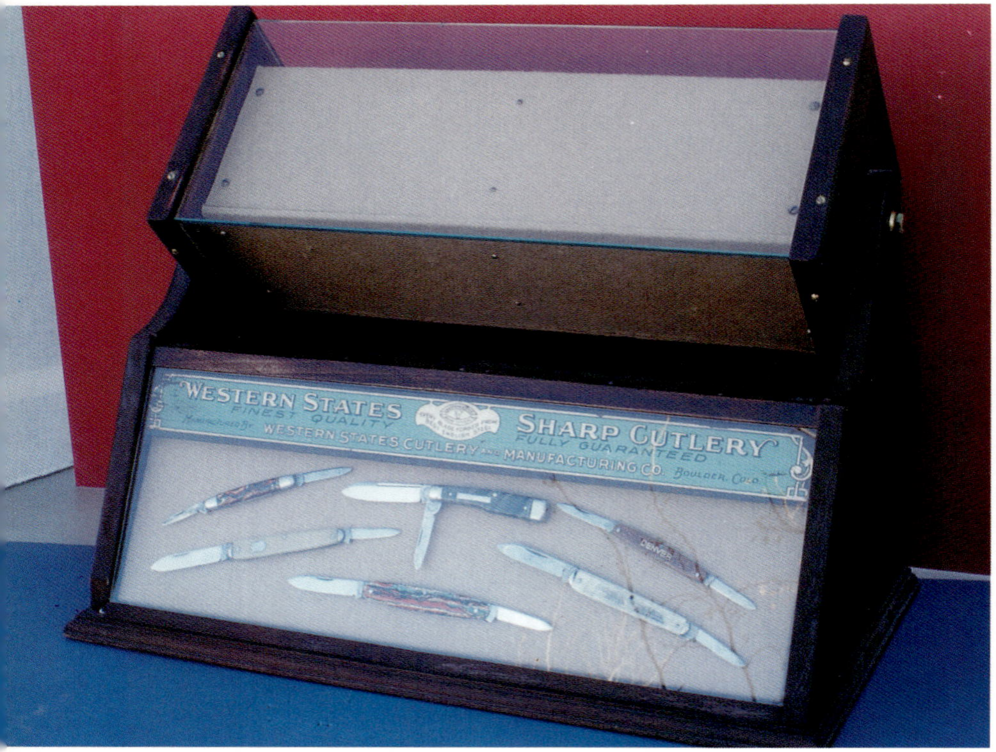

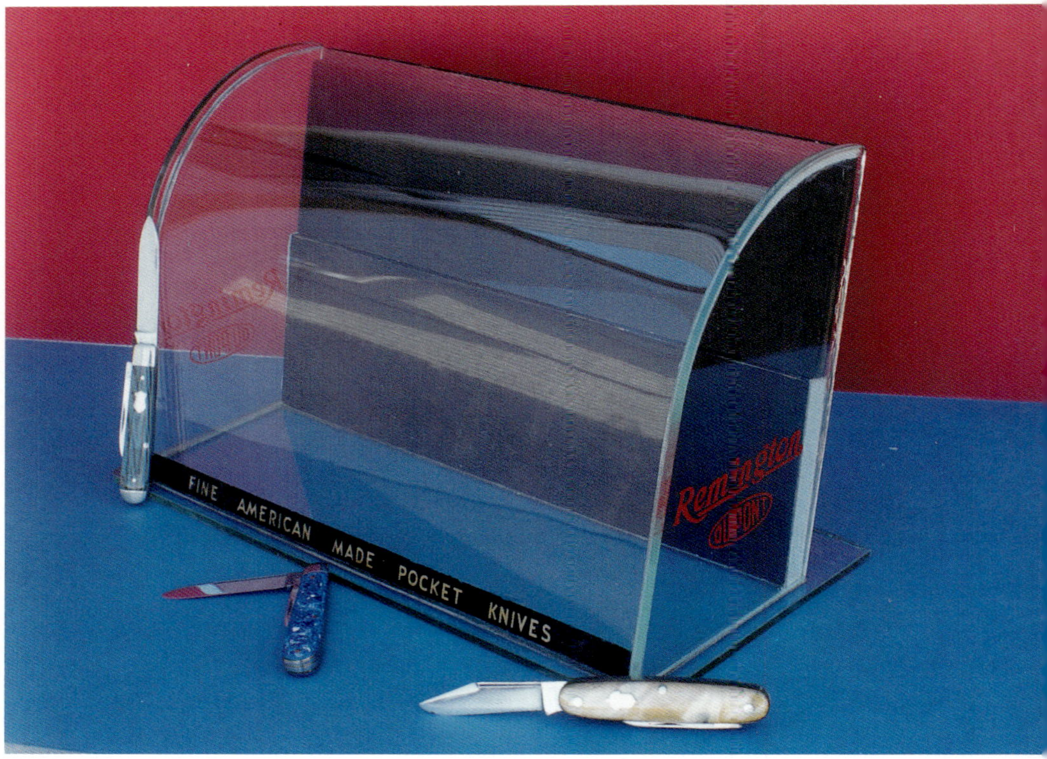

Above: One of the rarest cutlery showcases in existence, this tabletop model was made for the Western States Cutlery and Manufacturing Company originally located in Boulder, Colorado. Its uniqueness lies in its design. The top portion of the showcase has four separate panels, all of which were originally filled with knives, each individually wired onto the background board. The top portion of the showcase revolves 360°around the metal pins on each end. The bottom portion of the showcase clearly shows the Western States decal and six original Western States pocketknives. Visitors to the local hardware store could stand in front of this showcase and spin the top portion to see the various knives wired in the individual panels. Additional cutlery stock was stored in a lockable drawer located behind the bottom glass panel. According to top cutlery collectors across the United States, only about three or four of these showcases still exist with the top rotating portion intact. Recent cutlery auctions have helped set the price of this showcase between $750 and $1000.

Above right: Another very unique glass showcase with an outstanding cutlery name. This curved-glass showcase was made for the Remington Cutlery Company. The lettering on the bottom front advertises "Fine American Made Pocket Knives," with the side panels showing the "Remington/Dupont" lettering. The back portion of the showcase is black-painted wood. A small spring holds the door against the glass sides. Even the bottom of the showcase is glass. This showcase dates from the 1920s, and probably held one dozen Remington pocketknives in an upright card or container. The value of this very rare curved-glass showcase is $200–250.

Right: This wooden showcase was designed to be placed on the top of a counter in a hardware store. It was made to house "Imperial" knives. Like other wooden showcases with glass fronts, it is becoming very rare, especially with original painted lettering and real wood construction. Value of this showcase would be $90–120 without knives.

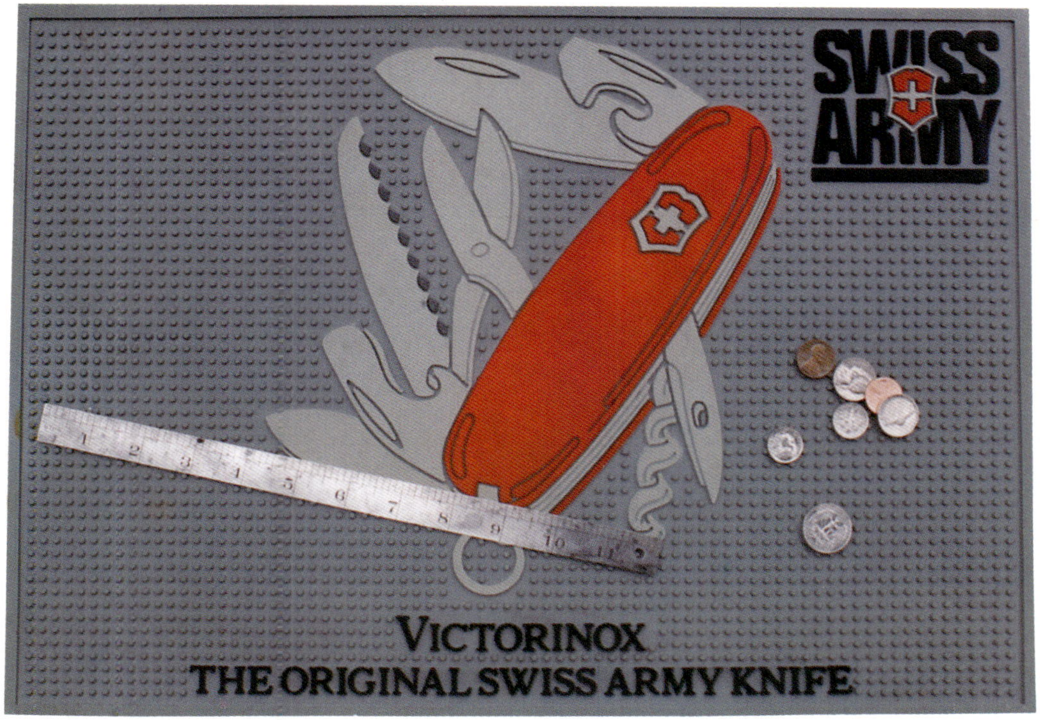

Left: Change mats are used by many companies to place the customer's change on to avoid scratching the glass showcase countertop. It is quite large, approximately 14 by 16 inches, and is composed of tiny raised bumps, so that change could be easily picked up. These mats were also used to place knives on for customer examination. They were made by a variety of old knife companies, and are a unique addition to any collection. This mat, made by Victorinox is of recent production, and is valued at $20–25, because of its cutlery advertisement, complex pattern, and three-color design.

Below left: This uniquely designed knife was produced in the United States in the 1940s, during an era informally known as the "streamline" era. The sleek metal passenger train called the "Streamliner" (shown in the photograph) is only one of a myriad of products ranging from toasters and blenders to chrome kitchens and automobiles which were re-designed to reflect this new visionary design movement. Cutlery, like many other product lines, felt the need to upgrade and redesign their products to fit the desires of the country. This knife is an example of such an effort. The value of this mint knife is $50–60.

Below right: A closeup photograph of the *STREAMLINE* logo engraving deeply on the master blade of this Camillus two-bladed jack knife. The Camillus "sword brand" logo is etched as a tang stamp, with Camillus etched on the back of the blade, and a long pull on the master blade.

Right: This magazine ad appeared in 1920s magazines, and featured the famous Keen Kutter, two-bladed "EZ open" knife with bone handles. Appealing to the age group illustrated in the ad, these knives were sometimes offered as "incentive" knives for magazine subscriptions. Properly matted and framed, original ads have a value of $35.

Far right: Typical advertisements found in 1920s and 1930s popular magazines. This ad was found in *American Boy* magazine. It featured the famous Marbles "Woodcraft" knife, as well as scout pattern tool knife, and pocketknife with chain attached. The knives featured in this advertisement were popular models with young boys.

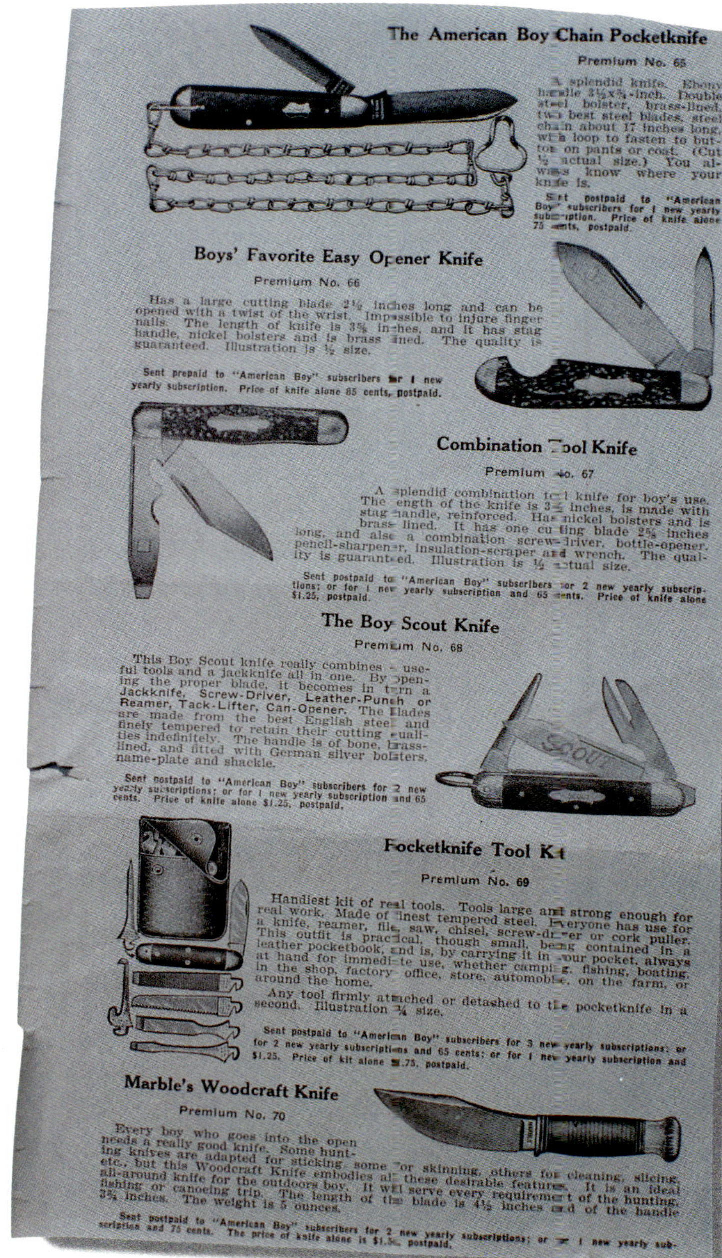

The American Boy Chain Pocketknife

Premium No. 65

A splendid knife. Ebony handle 3½x¾-inch. Double steel bolster, brass-lined, two best steel blades, steel chain about 17 inches long, with loop to fasten to button on pants or coat. (Cut ½ actual size.) You always know where your knife is.

Sent postpaid to "American Boy" subscribers for 1 new yearly subscription. Price of knife alone 75 cents, postpaid.

Boys' Favorite Easy Opener Knife

Premium No. 66

Has a large cutting blade 2½ inches long and can be opened with a twist of the wrist. Impossible to injure finger nails. The length of knife is 3⅝ inches, and it has stag handle, nickel bolsters and is brass lined. The quality is guaranteed. Illustration is ½ size.

Sent prepaid to "American Boy" subscribers for 1 new yearly subscription. Price of knife alone 85 cents, postpaid.

Combination Tool Knife

Premium No. 67

A splendid combination tool knife for boy's use. The length of the knife is 3½ inches, is made with stag handle, reinforced. Has nickel bolsters and is brass lined. It has one cutting blade 2⅝ inches long, and also a combination screw-driver, bottle-opener, pencil-sharpener, insulation-scraper and wrench. The quality is guaranteed. Illustration is ½ actual size.

Sent postpaid to "American Boy" subscribers for 2 new yearly subscriptions; or for 1 new yearly subscription and 65 cents. Price of knife alone $1.25, postpaid.

The Boy Scout Knife

Premium No. 68

This Boy Scout knife really combines 5 useful tools and a jackknife all in one. By opening the proper blade, it becomes in turn a Jackknife, Screw-Driver, Leather-Punch or Reamer, Tack-Lifter, Can-Opener. The blades are made from the best English steel and finely tempered to retain their cutting qualities indefinitely. The handle is of bone, brass-lined, and fitted with German silver bolsters, name-plate and shackle.

Sent postpaid to "American Boy" subscribers for 2 new yearly subscriptions; or for 1 new yearly subscription and 65 cents. Price of knife alone $1.25, postpaid.

Pocketknife Tool Kit

Premium No. 69

Handiest kit of real tools. Tools large and strong enough for real work. Made of finest tempered steel. Everyone has use for a knife, reamer, file, saw, chisel, screw-driver or cork puller. This outfit is practical, though small, being contained in a leather pocketbook, and is, by carrying it in your pocket, always at hand for immediate use, whether camping, fishing, boating, in the shop, factory, office, store, automobile, on the farm, or around the home.

Any tool firmly attached or detached to the pocketknife in a second. Illustration ¾ size.

Sent postpaid to "American Boy" subscribers for 3 new yearly subscriptions; or for 2 new yearly subscriptions and 65 cents; or for 1 new yearly subscription and $1.25. Price of kit alone $1.75, postpaid.

Marble's Woodcraft Knife

Premium No. 70

Every boy who goes into the open needs a really good knife. Some hunting knives are adapted for sticking, some for skinning, others for cleaning, slicing, etc., but this Woodcraft Knife embodies all these desirable features. It is an ideal all-around knife for the outdoors boy. It will serve every requirement of the hunting, fishing or canoeing trip. The length of the blade is 4½ inches and of the handle 3¾ inches. The weight is 5 ounces.

Sent postpaid to "American Boy" subscribers for 2 new yearly subscriptions; or for 1 new yearly subscription and 75 cents. The price of knife alone is $1.50, postpaid.

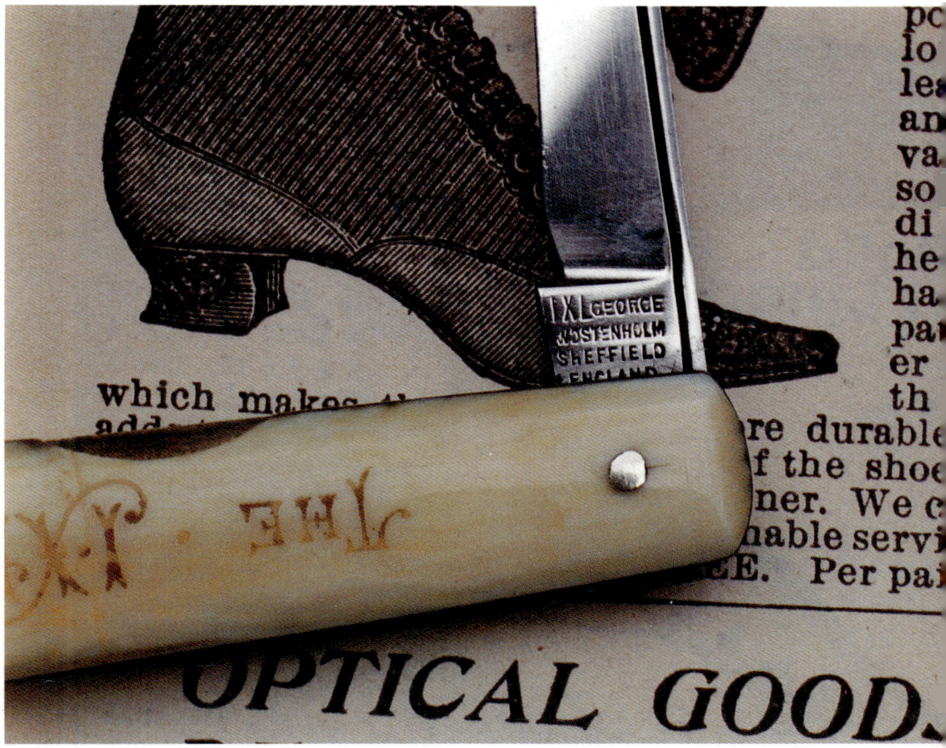

Above left: Cutlery Companies often do their own advertising by placing the name of the cutlery company on the sides of the knife itself. This "corn knife" was made by the "I*XL, George Wostenholm Company," located in Sheffield England. Corn knives were made specifically for the purpose of cutting corns off the feet of women who wore small shoes, as shown behind the knife. These knives were made with specially-tempered steel, which would retain the sharpness necessary for this type of procedure.

Above right: A closeup of the "I*XL" advertising knife shows the Wostenholm tang stamping. Normally, you would have to open the blades of the knife to see the manufacturer's name on the tang portion of the blade. This one announces the manufacturer on the celluloid sides. Value is based on the rather rare knife style, excellent condition, and ornate script advertising. Value is $40–45.

Left: All brands of cutlery were shipped to distributors and retailers in colorful boxes, which advertised the knives contained in the boxes. These boxes are so popular that some cutlery companies have began to reproduce these old box advertisements to house recent reproductions of earlier models (W. R. Case). Most included in this photo are old original boxes. Prices on the boxes add to the value as they help date the box. Value is $15–35 per box for originals, depending on condition and company name.

Top: Cutlery cards were used to wire knives on and were stood up on countertops as sales displays. These are from the "I*XL, George Wostenholm Cutlery Company," and date from the early 1900s to the 1930s. A single knife shows the various sizes which range from three to four inches up to larger cards which are up to eight by thirteen inches. The price of the knife would be inked into the white circles. Value ranges from $8–10 for the smaller cards, up to $20 for the larger cards.

Bottom: One of George Wostenholm's specialty items was the production of numerous specialty knives with "hawkbill" blades designed for working on plantations. These knives were shipped all over the world, including India and Africa—as much was under British rule. These cards are colorfully designed to attract the customer's eye, and are rare in mint condition. Value $12–20.

Left: Some of these cards were wired full of various knives, and placed in the bottom of glass showcases. This one is almost fifteen inches in length, and is shown with a regular knife for comparison. Value in mint condition is $25–35.

Below left: These small french ivory celluloid plaques were attached to the front of small oak cutlery showcases. In all probability, the "I*XL Cutlery Company" made both the knives and the showcases to put them in. These date from the early 1900s, and are rare in unused mint condition. Value, because of the rarity and condition, is $25–30 each.

Below right: Opening knife blades for eight hours or more each day was a killer on thumbnails, so cutlers developed various "knife openers" to assist them in opening blades with strong springs. Later, knife openers were made and stamped by a variety of companies, and were given away to customers as an advertising gimmick. Although reproductions have been made by Remington and Winchester (shown here), original openers like the Western States Cutlery Company opener shown are quite rare, and are worth up to $50–75. In addition to those mentioned above, knife blade openers were made by Robeson, Queen, Ulster, Challenge, Cattaraugus, and a host of others.

Top: This unique advertising shield is found on a two-bladed serpentine jack produced by Utica Cutlery Company. The "featherlight" advertisement was patented by Utica to be used originally on their lightweight girl scout knives. Although later girl scout knives with clear handles over green liners can be easily found in the $15–20 range, the girl scout knives using this mottled green celluloid are quite rare, and can be priced as much as $40 or more. Value of this jack knife with green celluloid and featherlight shield is $30–40.

Bottom: These interesting key chains were apparently made as giveaway items by the Primble Cutlery Company, Louisville, Kentucky. Made of jigged bone (the same material used in knife handles), these knives have the round Primble logo inset into them like those found on knives. Because of their rarity and close association to a famous cutlery brand, these keyrings are worth $30–40 each.

XII.
HUNTING AND FISHING

Top: One of the finest examples of advertising cutlery is this knife made by the old KA-BAR Cutlery Company of Olean, New York. This two-bladed fishing knife is handled in jigged black celluloid, and features not only a master blade, but a second blade containing a hook degorger and fish scaler. In addition, the left side of the celluloid handles contains a small sharpening stone for sharpening fishing hooks.

Bottom: A closeup photograph shows the *Field and Stream* etching on the master blade of this famous fishing knife. This knife was probably given away to customers who purchased a year's subscription to *Field and Stream* magazine, or was sold to subscribers for a small sum of money. It was made in the 1930s by KA-BAR, one of the most collectible knife names. The original *Field and Stream* etching on the master blade indicates that this knife is in pristine mint condition. Given these factors, this knife would be valued at $175–225. This stamping, with all capital letters in the word "KA-BAR" was started in 1923.

This KA-BAR fishing knife, known to knife collectors as a "Texas toothpick," clearly shows the two blades most often contained in this specialized knife. The first is a long, tapered blade used for cleaning fish. The second blade is a combination fishhook degorger and scale remover blade.

KA-BAR Advertising Knives Sport "Zane Grey" Endorsement

Any ranking of cutlery companies known to produce outstanding products almost always includes the KA-BAR Cutlery Company of Olean, New York at the top. Started in Tidioute, PA. around the turn of the century, as the Union Razor Company, it quickly became Union Cutlery Company in 1909. The first appearance of the famous KA-BAR stamping (with all letters capitalized), did not appear until the year 1929.

KA-BAR Cutlery Company produced perhaps the largest variety of hunting knives, (both pocket and sheath), military knives, and fishing knives of any cutlery company in the United States. Outstanding examples of these knives, frequently handled in stag or jigged bone, usually bear the KA-BAR stampings on the tang of the blade.

Two of the most famous and eagerly sought-after knives were the KA-BAR fly fishing knife, and the KA-BAR regular fishing knife. The fly fishing knife was handled in yellow celluloid, and contained a variety of specialized blades designed for the fly fisherman. Among the tools included in this knife was a master blade, scissors for cutting fly leader and for trimming fly hackles, a pointed needle punch for untying fly line knots, and file for sharpening hooks. The yellow celluloid made this knife easily seen if accidentally dropped into the water. In addition, it sported a bail for attaching it to a fishing vest.

The second knife, also handled in yellow celluloid for easy visibility, was the KA-BAR fishing knife. This style was called a "Texas toothpick"—a long knife (almost 5 inches) with two blades. The first blade was a long master blade, used for skinning and cleaning fish. The second blade was a combination fish scaler and hook degorger blade. In addition, a small sharpening stone was inlaid into the side of the celluloid so that dull hooks could be easily honed.

With the Great Depression in full swing, KA-BAR saw its share of the limited cutlery market on the decline, and decided to try to influence customer purchasing preferences through advertising. It was at this time that a unique partnership formed between KA-BAR Cutlery Company and Mr. Zane Grey. Grey was known worldwide, not only as a writer of outdoor and western fiction books, but also as a world class fisherman of some note.

A closeup of the KA-BAR fishing knife shows more accurately the deep color of the yellow celluloid. The knife was designated by the KA-BAR Cutlery Company as a T29, the number shown in red on the side of the knife. In addition, the photo shows the hook-sharpening stone embedded in the knife scales. Finally, the small hole at the end of the knife opposite the blade was used to straighten bent fish hooks.

The most important feature of this knife is not the knife itself but the advertisement it bears. "Endorsed by Zane Grey" is the important etching proudly proclaimed on the side of the blade. The boldness of the etching is indicative of the mint condition of this knife. In this condition, its value is $200–250.

As a writer, Zane Grey authored some sixty-six novels, most of which sold over one million copies. Perhaps the best known single title was *Riders of the Purple Sage,* published in 1912. In addition, Mr. Grey authored *The Last of the Plainsmen, The Spirit of the Border, The Call of the Canyon, Wildfire, Tales of Swordfish and Tuna,* and *Code of the West,* which was completed in 1934.

In addition to his prowess as a writer, Grey proved to be an outstanding sport fisherman, once holding ten world championship fishing records. With his annual salary from book sales was in the millions, he was able to travel to such exotic places as the Mexican Peninsula, Baja, South America, and Australia to pursue trophy-sized deep-sea fish. Certainly, some of his book titles attest to his "love affair" with fishing.

What better advertising for fishing cutlery than Mr. Zane Grey, world famous author and champion fisherman? Apparently KA-BAR approached Grey and asked him to endorse several fishing knives in return for cutlery samples to use during fishing expeditions. After reaching an acceptable agreement, Grey allowed KA-BAR to etch his name on the master blades of their fishing knives. Thus the "endorsed by Zane Grey" knives were born.

Zane Grey died in 1939, approximately seven years after the yellow fish knife was produced with his endorsement, but certainly provided KA-BAR with a "larger than life" folk hero as their cutlery spokesman. It could be easily proven that the exciting Zane Grey novels provided much-needed relief for the millions of Americans suffering the tremendously hard times associated with the 1930s Depression.

In today's advertising subculture, celebrity endorsements are almost a necessity. Everything from cereal to automobiles seems to be touted by someone "famous." It is interesting that, although we think of these celebrity endorsements as something out of the most recent television era, Zane Grey was certainly one of the first celebrities to endorse a product—in this case fishing knives.

As an advertising collectible, the Zane Grey KA-BAR fish knives cannot be beaten. Since the "endorsed by Zane Grey" blade etch appears on the master blade—the blade which is used most frequently—those knives which have a very pronounced blade etching can be rated in mint or near-mint condition. In addition, fish knives as a collectible are just now coming of age. Outstanding examples of both sheath and pocketknives designed for the fishing advocate can be found with a wide variety of company stampings etched on the tang of the master blade.

Top: In addition to fishing knives known as "Texas toothpicks," KA-BAR made specialized fly fishing knives, also endorsed by the famous sportsman Zane Grey. Handled like the toothpicks, in bright yellow celluloid for easy visibility, this knife also bears the "Zane Grey" endorsement on the master blade.

Bottom: A closeup of the KA-BAR fly fishing knife. This photo shows the long, pointed needle-blade used to untie knots from fly line. In addition, this knife contained a scissors for trimming fly hackle, a file, and a screwdriver built into the end. Its value seems to go up each year, with $300–400 not an outrageous price to pay for examples with clear Zane Grey endorsement, mint condition, and full blades.

Left: Sheath knives are rarely used as advertisers, but this large skinner, made by Buck, was used to advertise "Ambush," a type of ammunition. A skinning knife is an appropriate knife style to advertise this product, which would be seen specifically by hunters. Value is $40–50 with sheath. Buck knives in general are presently underpriced, and many valuable examples are still to be found.

Below left: This modern lockback was made by custom maker Al Mar. The knife is an advertiser for a variety of hunting and gun equipment including Weaver (gun sights), Outers (hunting clothing and equipment), Speer (rifle cartridges), and others. It is a finely made knife, with a good maker's stamp. It is valued at $50–60, perhaps more because lockback knives are a premium.

Below right: Produced by Kutmaster, this muskrat pattern knife is identified by its two extremely thin blades. Used for skinning muskrats or other trapped animals, it is thought to be named after its resemblance to a muskrat's tail. "Blake and Lamb," a company which produces animal traps and trapping equipment used this unique knife style to advertise their product. The value is $25–30, partially because it is handled in a plastic material called delrin, and because it shows the beginnings of rust and corrosion.

Top: Knife/axe combinations containing advertising are extremely rare. This set, complete with leather sheaths, was made by the Western Cutlery Company. Used primarily by hunters, sportsmen, and campers, it is a valuable tool set for the outdoorsman. Knife/axe combinations have been made by a number of companies including Case, KA-BAR, and Western.

Bottom: A closeup photograph of the advertisement embossed into the leather sheath reads "Cabela's." Cabela's is a world-famous sporting goods store, selling all types of camping supplies, guns, fishing rods, tents, boats, and everything else for those who enjoy the outdoors. Although this set was made in the 1980s, it has a value of $70–80.

XIII. MISCELLANEOUS

This unique cutlery advertiser was made by Ben Chon, (a.k.a. "Jack Knife Ben") in the 1920s. Uniquely designed to castrate cattle, it contains a spey blade and a sharpened castrating "hook" to cut the cord. Jack Knife Ben knives are very hard to find, especially in good condition, and are valued at $125–150 each.

A macro photograph of the tang stamping on the Jack Knife Ben, Chicago castrating knife. In addition to the name being stamped into the all metal handles, it is tang stamped on both blades with "Jack Knife Ben, Chicago."

Unique Story Surrounds Chicago Knife Salesman

A comparison photo of two castrating knives. The larger was made by Kutmaster, a more common stamping, and the smaller was made for Jack Knife Ben by a variety of companies. Both are made of stainless steel, necessary because these knives were frequently cleaned in water after use. The Kutmaster is valued at $25–30 in mint, unsharpened condition.

The time period was the late 1880s, and the place was the teeming acres located just south of Chicago's downtown. Although generally avoided by Chicago's "upper crust," this expansive area, the Chicago Stockyards, was one of the most important commerce centers in this bustling metropolis. Because of Chicago's unique central location, size, and industrial capacity, and the extensive crisscross of rail lines which traveled in all directions across the United States, seemingly everything started in Chicago.

As a result of this extensive rail network, recently expanded processing capabilities, and the influx of thousands of new immigrants, Chicago seemed destined to fulfill its destiny as one of the major production centers in the United States. Livestock was only one of the products which flowed through Chicago's south side, with tens of thousands of head arriving by rail each day. Into massive holding pens and yards these cattle were herded, to be sold, slaughtered, and packaged to meet the growing demand of urban areas and homesteaders moving west.

It was this same immense stockyard and rail complex that greeted Benjamin Chon, who arrived in Chicago with nothing but the clothing on his back and $8.00 in his pocket. Although the sound and dust that greeted him were enough to discourage all but the most persistent, it was the smell which drove most visitors from the area: that terrible, lingering odor of cattle enclosed in pens with tons of manure. If that alone was not enough, there was also the unforgettable stench of the meat processing plants, the odor which stayed on the bodies of workers even after showering.

For Ben Chon, however, this strange mixture of cattle buyers, ranchers, processors, and farmers together provided what turned out to be a winning business proposition. Walking along the myriad of pens, Chon noticed that these cattlemen used pocketknives almost constantly. Everyone here needs a good knife, he reasoned. Whether it was for cleaning boots, marking tally numbers, cutting rope, ear notches, or plugs of tobacco, a stout pocketknife with several different blades was a true friend and constant companion to cattlemen.

With these thoughts in mind, Chon purchased several dozen pocketknives with his eight dollars and set up shop. His "shop" was limited to the top of an old barrel, and his "showcase" was a small cigar box which held his knives. Standing next to one of the walkways which ran along the stockyard pens, Chon's business blossomed. Selling these knives at 25 cents each, he sold out quickly and went into downtown Chicago to get new stock. The ones he choose were of good quality, usually 3- or 4-bladed premium stockman knives with bone handles. With a supply of good knives and the gift of gab, Chon quickly depleted his remaining stock in short order.

Although Chon was frequently harassed by the rail police and local sheriff, and was told to move on, his business ventures grew, and he soon began to sell from a small shack located beside the stockyards. Chon never sold less than 40 knives per day, and once told a friend that he sold over 700 knives on a single record day. With this capital in hand he began to handle other merchandise, like straight razors, jewelry, diamonds, and leather goods—items he knew that men away from home and loved ones would need and appreciate.

It was at this time that Chon started ordering knives from the famous local Chicago hardware distributor, Hibbard, Spencer and Bartlett, whose slogan, "Our Very Best," was etched in a variety of products from oil cans to axe heads. Hibbard, Spencer, and Bartlett, who later became the world famous "Tru Value" Hardware conglomerate, did not make their own knives, but bought them from several large manufacturers. These included Napanoch Cutlery, Utica Cutlery, Schrade Cutlery, Ulster Knife Company, and Camillus Cutlery Company. All of these major cutlery producers stamped the knife styles they produced with either their own stamps or the tang stamp requested by the customer.

With his reputation firmly established, Ben began to have knives stamped with his own special logo. The logo he first used was the now-famous "Jack Knife Ben." Later, several other variations of this logo were used, including Jack Knife Ben Union Stockyards, Jack Knife Ben Handy Dandy, Jack Knife Ben-Chicago. These knives were stamped on the tang of the master blade, and were often stamped in the sides of the metal knife handles. These stampings were indicators of Ben's insistence on a quality product.

By 1925, "Jack Knife Ben" had an income reported to be in the hundreds of thousands of dollars each year, and his reputation spread throughout the country. He once quipped that he knew more farmers than anyone in the country. His regard for quality and honesty encouraged many people to buy an official "Jack Knife Ben" pocketknife. Supposedly, former Presidents Warren Harding and Calvin Coolidge both owned knives bearing the Jack Knife Ben stamping.

Jack Knife Ben, a.k.a. Benjamin Chon, is a tribute to American ingenuity, in a time where money was scarce and morals were loose. Excellent examples of this very rare knife stamping can be valued from $150.00 to $200.00. Jack Knife Ben is an advertising success story which belongs in every advertising publication.

Top. This six-bladed utility knife contains not only two cutting blades, but also a punch, corkscrew, can opener, and cap lifter. Made by Gustasf Spitzer in Solingen, Germany, it could have been made as early as the 1930s. The word "Continental" inlaid into the slick black celluloid is an advertisement for an unknown company. Because of its mint condition, six blades, and striking black with silver inlay, it is valued as $75–85.

Bottom: This small knife with fancy bolsters is supposedly a reproduction of the knife carried by George Washington. Washington's signature is etched into the side of this celluloid-handled knife. The shape of the single blade would make this knife usable for sharpening quills to be used as writing pens. Made by Camillus, it bears the four-line stamping made during the 1940s. Uniquely designed, it has a value of $40–45.

Above: Carl Schlieper Cutlery, started in 1769, was one of the earliest and finest cutlery companies in Germany. This metal-sided utility knife is quite small at only 3 inches in length, (normal utility knives are 3½ inches to 3¾ inches) This small size illustrates the craftsmanship necessary to fit six blades in a small space and still provide clearance for them all. The trademark for Schlieper is the "Eye Brand," seen clearly inscribed on the side.

Right: This knife is included because it is an "advertiser" for the craft of traditional blacksmithing and metal forging, as illustrated with the picture of the blacksmith and the various products he forges. The finished products include a metal shovel head, axe head, and several specialized knives used in the harvesting of sugar cane, bamboo and tall grasses. This knife is actually an advertisement for the cutlery industry. Its superb construction and unique advertisement give this knife a value of $150–200.

Above left: This very unique advertising piece commemorates both "Christmas" and "New Years." Produced by W. H. Morley and Sons, a wholesale brand out of Germany, it was produced between 1913 and 1927. Handled in wonderful old yellow french ivory, its unique message, age, and unsharpened condition help to raise its value to $50–60.

Above right: Unlike most knives which featured solid nickel-silver bolsters at each end, this pen knife was made with "birdseye" rivets. These were necessary to prevent the knife from pulling apart at the blade ends as the knife was used. The Morley "clover" trademark is seen on both pictures.

Left: The *R.M.S. Aquitania* was a steamship built in the early 1900s. Used in both World War I and World War II as a troop transport ship, it was a four-stacked cruise ship, in the same class as the *Lusitania*. The knife was produced by Forman Cutlery, Sheffield England. This particular knife was probably hand-engraved, perhaps by a servicemen or jeweler and presented to a member of the ship's crew. The handles are french ivory celluloid, and the knife has a value in the $40–50 range.

White celluloid provides the background for the nickel-silver ship inlay which takes up most of the knife. Extremely fine detail marks the ship named the *Oslofjord*. My assumption is that this is a pleasure ship, taking tourists around the various ports in Norway. Because of the unique inlay, this knife is worth \$45–55 as a tourist collectible.

This four-bladed lobster pattern knife was made over 100 years ago. Although the tang is stamped "KB," no maker's name is visible. Below the gentleman's feet is the word "Leksand," a town in Sweden. This knife commemorates that small town.

A closeup view of the Leksand commemorative knife showing the gold wash which was originally applied to the pants and around the background area. This knife shows men and women in traditional costume, working in the fields.

The back side of the knife shows a lady dressed in traditional costume. Both the man and the woman are holding what appears to be a hoe or tool used to weed agricultural products. These are all clues to the mystery behind this unique knife. The value is $70–80 because of fine craftsmanship, and unique story.

Above: A metal-sided pen knife with corkscrew is adorned with fancy engraved scrollwork and the name "Eskilstuna." In addition, the tang stamping contains the same name and another: "Emil Lsson." I assume that the names refer to the maker and the town where this interesting knife was made. Like most fancy metal jacks, this knife is worth $45–55.

Above right: This photograph shows the "Eskilstuna" knife with the corkscrew in the open position. Looking at the craftsmanship, this knife would be made during the first part of the twentieth century.

Right: This unique cutlery item is shaped like a silver dollar. Opening like two wings are the two enclosed blades. The uniqueness of this knife lies in the five-year perpetual calendar attached as a part of this knife. By twisting the outer dial, you can line up the correct date for each month from the years 1942 to 1947. These calendar knives are very rare and have a value of $50–60.

BIBLIOGRAPHY

Bardy, Ed, *Advertising with a Sharp Edge,* Traverse City, Michigan: The Latch String, 1972.

Bezdek, Richard H. *American Swords and Swordmakers*, Boulder, Colorado, Paladin Press, 1994.

Hake, Ted, *Hake's Guide to Advertising Collectibles*, Radnor, Pennsylvania, Wallace Homestead Book Co., 1992.

Levine, Bernard, *Levine's Guide to Knives and Their Values*, 4th Edition, Iola, Wisconsin: Krause Publications, Inc., 1997.

Petretti, Allen, *Petretti's Coca Cola Price Guide*, 10th Edition, Dubuque, Iowa, Antique Trader Books, 1997.

Platts, Harvey, *The Knife Makers Who Went West*, Longmont, Colorado, Longs Peak Press, 1978.

Room, Adrian, *NTC Dictionary of Trade Name Origins*, Lincolnwood, Illinois, NTC Business Books, 1994.

Sargent, Jim, *American Premium Guide to Knives and Razors, 4th Edition*, Florence, Alabama: Books Americana, 1995.

Smokey Mountain Knife Works, Classic Collectibles: J.P. Huddleston Collection, Sevierville, Tennessee, Smokey Mountain Knife Works, 1989.

Voyles, Bruce, J., *The International Blade Collectors Association Price Guide to Antique Knives, Second Edition*, Iola, Wisconsin: Krause Publications, Inc., 1995.

Wolff, Jim, 1997, *Remington Premium Knives*, Knife World Magazine, July, 1-7.